T0123680

An Analysis of

Bernard Bailyn's

The Ideological Origins of the American Revolution

Joshua Specht
With
Etienne Stockland

Published by Macat International Ltd
24:13 Coda Centre, 189 Munster Road, London SW6 6AW.

Distributed exclusively by Routledge
2 Park Square, Milton Park, Abingdon, Oxon OX14 4RN
711 Third Avenue, New York, NY 10017, USA

Routledge is an imprint of the Taylor & Francis Group, an informa business

Copyright © 2017 by Macat International Ltd
Macat International has asserted its right under the Copyright, Designs and Patents Act
1988 to be identified as the copyright holder of this work.

The print publication is protected by copyright. Prior to any prohibited reproduction, storage in
a retrieval system, distribution or transmission in any form or by any means, electronic, mechanical, recording or otherwise, permission should be obtained from the publisher or where
applicable a license permitting restricted copying in the United Kingdom should be obtained
from the Copyright Licensing Agency Ltd, Barnard's Inn, 86 Fetter Lane, London EC4A 1EN, UK.

The ePublication is protected by copyright and must not be copied, reproduced, transferred,
distributed, leased, licensed or publicly performed or used in any way except as specifically
permitted in writing by the publishers, as allowed under the terms and conditions under which
it was purchased, or as strictly permitted by applicable copyright law. Any unauthorised distribution or use of this text may be a direct infringement of the authors and the publishers' rights
and those responsible may be liable in law accordingly.

www.macat.com
info@macat.com

Cataloguing in Publication Data
A catalogue record for this book is available from the British Library.
Library of Congress Cataloguing-in-Publication Data is available upon request.
Cover illustration: Etienne Gilfillan

ISBN 978-1-912302-43-7 (hardback)
ISBN 978-1-912128-47-1 (paperback)
ISBN 978-1-912281-31-2 (e-book)

Notice

The information in this book is designed to orientate readers of the work under analysis,
to elucidate and contextualise its key ideas and themes, and to aid in the development
of critical thinking skills. It is not meant to be used, nor should it be used, as a
substitute for original thinking or in place of original writing or research. References and
notes are provided for informational purposes and their presence does not constitute
endorsement of the information or opinions therein. This book is presented solely for
educational purposes. It is sold on the understanding that the publisher is not engaged
to provide any scholarly advice. The publisher has made every effort to ensure that
this book is accurate and up-to-date, but makes no warranties or representations with
regard to the completeness or reliability of the information it contains. The information
and the opinions provided herein are not guaranteed or warranted to produce particular
results and may not be suitable for students of every ability. The publisher shall not be
liable for any loss, damage or disruption arising from any errors or omissions, or from
the use of this book, including, but not limited to, special, incidental, consequential or
other damages caused, or alleged to have been caused, directly or indirectly, by the
information contained within.

CONTENTS

THE MACAT LIBRARY

The Macat Library is a series of unique academic explorations of seminal works in the humanities and social sciences – books and papers that have had a significant and widely recognised impact on their disciplines. It has been created to serve as much more than just a summary of what lies between the covers of a great book. It illuminates and explores the influences on, ideas of, and impact of that book. Our goal is to offer a learning resource that encourages critical thinking and fosters a better, deeper understanding of important ideas.

Each publication is divided into three Sections: Influences, Ideas, and Impact. Each Section has four Modules. These explore every important facet of the work, and the responses to it.

This Section-Module structure makes a Macat Library book easy to use, but it has another important feature. Because each Macat book is written to the same format, it is possible (and encouraged!) to cross-reference multiple Macat books along the same lines of inquiry or research. This allows the reader to open up interesting interdisciplinary pathways.

To further aid your reading, lists of glossary terms and people mentioned are included at the end of this book (these are indicated by an asterisk [*] throughout) – as well as a list of works cited.

Macat has worked with the University of Cambridge to identify the elements of critical thinking and understand the ways in which six different skills combine to enable effective thinking.
Three allow us to fully understand a problem; three more give us the tools to solve it. Together, these six skills make up the **PACIER** model of critical thinking. They are:

ANALYSIS – understanding how an argument is built
EVALUATION – exploring the strengths and weaknesses of an argument
INTERPRETATION – understanding issues of meaning

CREATIVE THINKING – coming up with new ideas and fresh connections
PROBLEM-SOLVING – producing strong solutions
REASONING – creating strong arguments

To find out more, visit **WWW.MACAT.COM.**

CRITICAL THINKING AND *THE IDEOLOGICAL ORIGINS OF THE AMERICAN REVOLUTION*

Primary critical thinking skill: CREATIVE THINKING
Secondary critical thinking skill: ANALYSIS

Historians of the American Revolution had always seen the struggle for independence either as a conflict sparked by heavyweight ideology, or as a war between opposing social groups acting out of self-interest.

In *The Ideological Origins of the American Revolution*, Bernard Bailyn begged to differ, re-examining familiar evidence to establish new connections that in turn allowed him to generate fresh explanations. His influential reconceptualizing of the underlying reasons for America's independence drive focused instead on pamphleteering – and specifically on the actions of an influential group of 'conspirators' who identified, and were determined to protect, a particularly American set of values. For Bailyn, these ideas could indeed be traced back to the ferment of the English Civil War – stemming from radical pamphleteers whose anti-authoritarian ideas crossed the Atlantic and embedded themselves in colonial ideology. Bailyn's thesis helps to explain the Revolution's success by pointing out how deep-rooted its founding ideas were; the Founding Fathers may have been reading Locke, but the men they led were inspired by shorter, pithier and altogether far more radical works. Only by understanding this, Bailyn argues, can we understand the passion and determination that allowed the rebel American states to defeat a global superpower.

ABOUT THE AUTHOR OF THE ORIGINAL WORK

Bernard Bailyn is an American historian and professor emeritus at
Harvard University, where he has spent his entire academic career. Born in
Connecticut in 1922, he published his first Pulitzer Prize-winning book,
The Ideological Origins of the American Revolution, in 1967 after studying over
400 revolutionary-era political pamphlets. Bailyn received a second
Pulitzer Prize for his 1986 work *Voyagers to the West: A Passage in the
Peopling of America on the Eve of the Revolution*. He has also become a key
figure in developing the new academic field of Atlantic history, a discipline
that studies the group of countries bordering the Atlantic Ocean as a
coherent unit.

ABOUT THE AUTHORS OF THE ANALYSIS

Etienne Stockland is researching a PhD in environmental history at
Columbia University.

ABOUT MACAT

GREAT WORKS FOR CRITICAL THINKING

Macat is focused on making the ideas of the world's great thinkers
accessible and comprehensible to everybody, everywhere, in ways that
promote the development of enhanced critical thinking skills.

It works with leading academics from the world's top universities to
produce new analyses that focus on the ideas and the impact of the most
influential works ever written across a wide variety of academic disciplines.
Each of the works that sit at the heart of its growing library is an enduring
example of great thinking. But by setting them in context – and looking
at the influences that shaped their authors, as well as the responses they
provoked – Macat encourages readers to look at these classics and
game-changers with fresh eyes. Readers learn to think, engage and
challenge their ideas, rather than simply accepting them.

'Macat offers an amazing first-of-its-kind tool for interdisciplinary learning and research. Its focus on works that transformed their disciplines and its rigorous approach, drawing on the world's leading experts and educational institutions, opens up a world-class education to anyone.'

Andreas Schleicher
Director for Education and Skills, Organisation for Economic Co-operation and Development

'Macat is taking on some of the major challenges in university education ... They have drawn together a strong team of active academics who are producing teaching materials that are novel in the breadth of their approach.'

Prof Lord Broers,
former Vice-Chancellor of the University of Cambridge

'The Macat vision is exceptionally exciting. It focuses upon new modes of learning which analyse and explain seminal texts which have profoundly influenced world thinking and so social and economic development. It promotes the kind of critical thinking which is essential for any society and economy. This is the learning of the future.'

Rt Hon Charles Clarke, former UK Secretary of State for Education

'The Macat analyses provide immediate access to the critical conversation surrounding the books that have shaped their respective discipline, which will make them an invaluable resource to all of those, students and teachers, working in the field.'

Professor William Tronzo, University of California at San Diego

WAYS IN TO THE TEXT

KEY POINTS

- Bernard Bailyn is an American historian, Pulitzer Prize*-winning author, and professor emeritus at Harvard University.

- In *Ideological Origins* (1967), Bailyn argues that the American Revolution* of 1775–83, a conflict fought by 13 British colonies to secure their independence from Britain, was not instigated by struggle between social classes but was, above all, a battle of political ideas and beliefs.

- Bailyn reveals the powerful—and previously unknown—influence of republican* pamphlets (leaflets written by those who wanted the young United States to govern itself, without a British monarch as head of state) on the thinking of colonists during the American Revolution.

Who is Bernard Bailyn?

Bernard Bailyn, the author of *The Ideological Origins of the American Revolution*, was born in the US city of Hartford, Connecticut, in 1922. As an undergraduate, he attended Williams College* in Massachusetts before serving in the US Army during World War II.* Afterward he studied at Harvard University, where he received his PhD in 1953, and began teaching there soon after. Bailyn became a full professor in 1961, and has remained at that institution for his entire career. At

Harvard, he studied under some of the most important historians and scholars of the 1950s, including Perry Miller,* Samuel Eliot Morison,* and Oscar Handlin,* all noted for their contribution to American history. From Miller, much of whose career was concerned with tracing the intellectual origins of American identity, Bailyn inherited a concern with the revolutionary era and a belief that the ideas of seventeenth-century English settlers left a profound imprint on American culture.

Like his mentors (notably Miller, who emphasized the decisive influence of the Christian Puritan* movement on American culture), Bailyn chiefly studied life in New England,* a region then considered key in understanding the colonial period. His ideas were also strongly influenced by his contact with intellectual historians and political theorists studying seventeenth- and eighteenth-century England. A central argument of *Ideological Origins* was that English radical political thought was central to revolutionary politics. While many scholars had examined English domestic politics, Bailyn's application of this literature to the American colonies was novel.[1] This highlights the nature of Bailyn's originality and influences: he seems to have read widely and developed an eye for introducing scholarship into new contexts.

What Does *Ideological Origins* Say?

The core question of Bailyn's *Ideological Origins* is: "What caused the American Revolution?"

At the time of publication, the academic consensus was that the Revolution was driven by social conflict. That is, it resulted from: first, rifts between the needs of the colonial settlers and the British government; second, disagreement among the different classes within the United States—capitalists* (roughly, those with the money to make investments and accrue profits), plantation owners, and farmers—over who should rule in the British government's place.

Although Bailyn agreed that the Revolution was radical, in that it fundamentally rewrote the nature of America, he argues that it was "not primarily a controversy between social groups undertaken to force changes in the organization of the society or the economy." Bailyn asserts that the Revolution was driven by *ideology*, stating that "the American Revolution was above all else an ideological, constitutional, political struggle."[2] He reconstructs these revolutionary ideas through a broad examination of political pamphlets that were widely circulated in both the United States and England throughout the revolutionary period (1765–83). The pamphlets were highly polemical* (that is, controversial and creating debate and disputes). They addressed important political issues and proposed responses to these issues.

Prior to *Ideological Origins*, it was generally believed that the ideas of the English philosopher John Locke* and the Enlightenment* were key to revolutionary ideology. The Enlightenment was an eighteenth-century movement that promoted science, liberty, and rationality over tradition and religion. Locke, one of its key thinkers, proclaimed that all men were born with inalienable rights.

Bailyn's work moves beyond this by finding a new, recurring strand of radical thought in these pamphlets. He explains that many of the revolutionary pamphlets warned of organized conspiracy against the liberty of the Thirteen Colonies (the founder states of the United States). Bailyn claims the pamphlets drew on a "peculiar strain of anti-authoritarianism bred in the upheaval of the English Civil War"*[3] (1642–51). In the seventeenth and early eighteenth centuries, Britain's anti-authoritarians believed that liberty was a central virtue of British society. They also maintained that constant political corruption threatened this liberty. Largely ignored in England at the time, these anti-authoritarian ideas resonated with the American colonists; when the British government attempted to exert more direct control over the colonies by increasing taxation in the 1760s and 1770s, it was perceived as a "deliberate assault launched surreptitiously by plotters against liberty both in England and in America."[4] Eventually the colonists decided that revolution was necessary to protect their society.

Bailyn's arguments fit well into the broader intellectual movement when it was published. One reviewer commented that Bailyn had "written the book that existing scholarship made inevitable."[5] However, it is crucial to recognize how successfully Bailyn managed to combine such a diverse set of scholarly ideas about the role of ideology in the Revolution. As a result, *Ideological Origins* became central to the emergence of a new understanding of the Revolution as inseparable from a set of republican ideas about how society should be organized (republicanism being the belief that the supreme power in any country should be held by the electorate, having no royal head of state).

Bailyn explains that these ideas became "centered on the fear of centralized power and rooted in the belief that free states are fragile and degenerate easily into tyrannies unless vigilantly protected by a free, knowledgeable, and uncorrupted electorate working through institutions that balance and distribute rather than concentrate power."[6] Because Bailyn's theory soon became the dominant framework for understanding early American political thought, *Ideological Origins* remained highly influential for decades after its publication. By emphasizing how ideas influenced a population's perception of events, Bailyn effectively shows how intellectual history*—the study of ideas in history—can be connected to mass action.

Why Does *Ideological Origins* Matter?

Bernard Bailyn's argument in *Ideological Origins* has been persuasive to (or at least considered plausible by) scholars from a wide range of ideological backgrounds. This is thanks in part to his emphasis on careful research and extensive documentation. Bailyn's work contrasts with the traditional accounts of the Revolution that are based on social conflict* (the struggle that occurs between different social groups for power), such as the influential historian Charles Beard's* *An Economic Interpretation of the Constitution of the United States* (1913). Such accounts would view the pamphlets and their claims as pure rhetoric* (that is, language intended to influence or persuade people). They would also argue that class conflicts are the force driving the pamphlets' claims. Bailyn's work provides a useful alternative to these accounts; while his arguments apply to the American Revolution, his emphasis on the relationship between ideas, perceptions, and events is effective for analyzing a range of literate cultures. This helps to explain its longstanding influence.

The book's enduring impact has been in two main areas. First, *Ideological Origins* was key to the emergence of the Republican Synthesis,* a new model for understanding early American history, which revolutionized academic understanding of the Revolution. The Republican Synthesis* movement held that a set of republican ideas characterized early American political thought, that these ideas included a suspicion of British authority, and a belief that political systems should be developed to check some of the central tensions that exist in any free political system. While this republican emphasis has since been somewhat overturned, the movement remains influential.

Second, Bailyn's revitalization of intellectual histories of the American Revolution and early republic remains a key aspect in the ongoing debate. Although the field of early American history has changed dramatically since the late 1960s, *Ideological Origins* remains a central text, and scholars today still study and debate Bailyn's approach.

More recent work that supports the traditional emphasis on social conflict, however, has highlighted a genuine difficulty with idea-centered explanations such as Bailyn's—a difficulty that had already been identified at the time *Ideological Origins* was published. How is it possible to determine whether rhetoric in pamphlets was a genuine expression of thought, or merely a way of justifying goals and desires that were, in fact, rooted in economic or social conflicts?

Finally, it is unsurprising that a book that is more than 40 years old has been thoroughly analyzed and critiqued. Despite being under attack from conflict-centered accounts, *Ideological Origins* remains influential to this day, and Bailyn's powerfully constructed arguments are still part of contemporary debates.

NOTES

1   Bernard Bailyn, *The Ideological Origins of the American Revolution* (Cambridge, MA: Belknap Press, 1992), XII.

2   Bailyn, *Ideological Origins*, XII.

3   Bailyn, *Ideological Origins*, XII.

4   Bailyn, *Ideological Origins*, 95.

5   Z. S. Fink, "Review of the Ideological Origins of the American Revolution," *Historical Journal* 11, no. 3 (1968): 588–90.

6   Bailyn, *Ideological Origins*, 323.

SECTION 1
INFLUENCES

MODULE 1
THE AUTHOR AND THE
HISTORICAL CONTEXT

KEY POINTS

- Bernard Bailyn's *Ideological Origins* remains a foundational work of early American intellectual history.

- Bailyn studied under Perry Miller,* one of the foremost intellectual historians (a scholar of ideas in history) of early America.

- *Ideological Origins* was published during the Cold War* (1947–91), a period of tension between communist Soviet Union* and capitalist United States and their respective allies, when Americans sought to establish the origins of the intellectual and ideological values that underpinned American democracy.

Why Read This Text?

First published in 1967, Bernard Bailyn's *The Ideological Origins of the American Revolution* became a key text in explaining the relationship between political and social ideas and the material causes of the American Revolution*—the conflict fought for the independence of the young United States from British rule. The book criticized the existing scholarship, which argued that the American Revolution was the consequence of class conflict. Instead, Bailyn advocates the "rather old-fashioned view the American Revolution was above all else an ideological, constitutional, political struggle and not primarily a controversy between social groups undertaken to force changes in the organization of the society or the economy."[1]

> 66 Within the last several decades a dramatic
> reorientation has taken place in interpretation of the
> Revolutionary and early national periods. This new
> perspective is the result of scholars' recognition of
> the vital function of republicanism in early American
> society ... more than any other historian, Bernard
> Bailyn was the progenitor of this new appreciation of
> republicanism. 99
>
> Robert E. Shalhope, "Republicanism and Early American Historiography"

At the time of publication, Bailyn was one of the foremost scholars of early American history and a professor at Harvard University. *Ideological Origins* dramatically increased his fame as the book earned him one of the highest prizes in the historical profession, the Bancroft Prize,* as well as one of the most prestigious general non-fiction prizes in the United States, the Pulitzer Prize.* Bailyn's work was so influential that his account was said to have "quickly established a new paradigm* [conceptual model] for interpreting the Revolution."[2] As the historian Robert E. Shalhope* remarked in a review of the field of research into early America, Bailyn was the "progenitor" (that is, the first person to think of, do, or begin something) of a "new appreciation of republicanism" that later characterized academic study in the field.

Author's Life
Born in Hartford, Connecticut, in the United States in 1922, Bernard Bailyn attended Williams College* in Western Massachusetts before serving in the US Army during World War II.* After the war, Bailyn enrolled at Harvard University, where he studied under some of the most important and influential historians and scholars of the 1950s, including Perry Miller and Oscar Handlin,* both noted for their

scholarship in American history. Shortly after receiving his PhD in 1953, Bailyn also began teaching at Harvard.

Bailyn immediately established himself as a leading authority in the field of early American history. He received the Pulitzer and Bancroft literary prizes for *Ideological Origins. The Ordeal of Thomas Hutchinson* (1974), a biography of the governor of Massachusetts during the American Revolution, received a National Book Award and Bailyn received a second Pulitzer Prize for his 1986 book *Voyagers to the West: A Passage in the Peopling of America on the Eve of the Revolution*, which examined the migration of British and Scottish farmers to colonial America in the 1770s.

Later in his career, Bailyn became a key figure in Atlantic history,* a historical subfield that studies the Atlantic rim* (the collective group of countries that border the Atlantic Ocean) as a coherent historical unit. Atlantic history also examines the flow of commodities, people, and ideas between the Atlantic rim countries of Europe, the coastal Americas, the Caribbean, and the African coast. Bailyn established a regular seminar on Atlantic history at Harvard University that promoted the study of this emerging field by allowing scholars to present original research on the subject.

Author's Background

Much of Bailyn's work must be understood in a Cold War context, especially the earlier editions of *Ideological Origins*. The Cold War was a period of intense political and economic rivalry, and sometimes open hostility, between the United States and the Soviet Union from around 1947 to 1991. This conflict brought a new emphasis to understanding American identity, and historians looked to the revolutionary period for the origins of this identity. Progressive* historians such as Charles Beard* stressed the importance of conflict between different social groups as the key driver of American history, from its origin to modern times. But in the 1950s and 1960s, other scholars embraced the consensus* view of American history. This consensus view argued that the key factor in America's development was not social conflict but the negotiation of shared core values, which bonded together this new society.

While the consensus account established by the political scientist Louis Hartz* in *The Liberal Tradition in America* (1955) was popular at the time Bailyn's book was published, this theory struggled to explain the diversity of political views throughout American history. This posed problems for a profession—and, more broadly, a country—searching for a celebratory core set of American values to contrast against the political philosophy of communism, the economic and social system on which the Soviet Union was founded.

Bailyn's groundbreaking book managed to revitalize the consensus view by providing a unifying set of anti-authoritarian attitudes in pre-Revolution America. His arguments provided a new set of values, both intellectual and ideological, to underpin American democracy in the context of an intensive military, economic, and cultural conflict with the Soviet Union.

NOTES

1 Bernard Bailyn, *The Ideological Origins of the American Revolution* (Cambridge, MA: Belknap Press, 1992), x.

2 Robert E. Shalhope, "Republicanism and Early American Historiography," *The William and Mary Quarterly* 39, no. 2 (1982): 335.

MODULE 2
ACADEMIC CONTEXT

KEY POINTS

- Bailyn's book was concerned with explaining the intellectual foundations and origins of the American Revolution.*

- Most previous intellectual accounts of the American Revolution emphasized the importance of the English philosopher John Locke* and other key philosophers of the period of intellectual history known as the Enlightenment.*

- Bailyn used pamphlet literature of the revolutionary period to examine how ordinary people, rather than political elites, understood the events of their time.

The Work in its Context

In 1967, when Bernard Bailyn published *The Ideological Origins of the American Revolution*, explanations for the American Revolution—the conflict in which the young United States fought Britain for its independence—fell into two broad camps. In the first were intellectual historians—scholars of ideas in history—who emphasized the importance of ideas; in the second were progressive* academics, who emphasized the role of conflict between social groups.

Bailyn's approach placed him firmly on the side of intellectual history* but the ideas he found most important—namely, radical English political thought—gave him a highly original perspective. It differed from the early focus on the English philosopher John Locke and the Enlightenment movement, whose ideologies emphasized abstract rights and rationality. By carefully studying the revolutionary

> ❝ When republicanism was revived by Bernard
> Bailyn, Gordon Wood, J. G. A Pocock, and many others
> in the late 1960s and early 1970, it came at a time
> when many historians were searching for theoretical
> alternatives to the consensus historiography that had
> been long dominated by Louis Hartz's model of liberal
> capitalism. ❞
>
> Steven J. Ross, "The Transformation of Republican Ideology"

pamphlets, Bailyn moved beyond abstract philosophies and, within the leaflets, identified more popular social and political thinking in the colonies.

The use of political pamphlets had become hugely popular in Britain during the English Civil War* of the 1640s (a conflict fought to settle the question of whether power should lie in the hands of the monarchy or in the hands of the institution of Parliament). In this new "public sphere," the British pamphlets showed that the public had widespread fears about an organized plot between the government and the Catholic Church* to take over England (England was then, or considered itself, a Protestant* nation; given the political importance of faith in Europe, the split of the Christian religion into these two branches led to deep political consequences in Europe). The British public also feared a descent into anarchy, and they took up arms accordingly. In *Ideological Origins*, Bailyn showed the similarities between these leaflets and the later American pamphlets, which warned that the Episcopal Church—the Church of England—and the British colonial administration were tyrannical forces, conniving to deprive Americans of their liberty. As a result, Bailyn produced both a highly original argument and one that he could later refer to as "rather old fashioned."[1]

Bailyn's broadening of revolutionary ideology was timely. It fit into a trend at that time of moving beyond high-level political or intellectual histories, toward the perspectives and importance of people from all classes and parts of society. In Bailyn's arguments, the ideas of the colonists on the street mattered as much as those of the members of the Continental Congress,* the governing body for the original 13 American colonies (established in 1774). In addition, Bailyn showed that Locke's treatises on the nature of government were not capable of explaining the full range of ideas that influenced the American Revolution—because colonists of *all* educational levels, not just the political elite, held revolutionary ideas.

Overview of the Field

Like his predecessors, Bailyn was fascinated by both the intellectual roots of the American Revolution and the roots of American identity, and *Ideological Origins* successfully addressed the key academic debates current at the time of publication. In addition, he resolved some questions about the earlier understandings of revolutionary political thought that had plagued academic historians. The political scientist Louis Hartz* and his followers had all emphasized the ideas of Locke in their works. But they had seemed unable to account for the pervasive anxiety of colonists regarding British measures, such as the increase in taxes that at the time would have seemed quite moderate. Bailyn's chief challenge was to resolve the problems in these earlier intellectual histories of the Revolution—and in *Ideological Origins*, he solved them capably.

The final noteworthy aspect of the intellectual environment of Bailyn's work was the place of New England* in early American historiography* (that is, the existing body of work in an academic field). The eastern region of New England had long been the focus of scholarship on early America, as Puritanism* was seen to have provided the intellectual basis for America's democratic and commercial society. Starting with Bailyn's mentor, the intellectual historian and Harvard professor Perry Miller,* scholars sought the origin of American identity in the sermons and ideas of New England preachers. One key figure was the Puritan Jonathan Edwards,* who sparked the evangelical movement known as the Great Awakening* that swept America and challenged the authority of the Protestant Church in the 1730s and 1740s. Bailyn continued this trend, and his work reflects a preference for New England sources. However, its intellectual history approach and its emphasis on Atlantic linkages— particularly Bailyn's focus on the circulation of English radical thought—played a role in moving scholarship beyond New England.

Academic Influences

Bailyn's ideas were also strongly influenced by his contact with intellectual historians and political theorists studying seventeenth- and eighteenth-century England, such as Perry Miller, Samuel Eliot Morison,* and Oscar Handlin.* A central contention of *Ideological Origins* was that English radical political thought dating back to the 1640s was central to American revolutionary politics. While many scholars had examined English domestic politics, Bailyn's application of this literature to the colonies was novel.[2] This highlights the nature both of Bailyn's originality and his influences: he seems to have read widely and developed an eye for introducing scholarship into new contexts.

Bailyn's book was timely. Published during the period of global tension known as the Cold War,* largely driven by the competing ideologies of the Soviet Union* and the United States, there was an emphasis on understanding American identity, and historians looked to the revolutionary period for the origins of this identity. The literature produced by these historians followed the consensus* approach to American history, which emphasized the negotiation of shared core values—often relating to freedom or liberty—as the key driver of America's formation and early history.

While this consensus view was already widely held when Bailyn wrote his text, scholars were increasingly struggling to account for the diversity of political views they had found throughout American history, which put the consensus theory in doubt. Bailyn's book successfully revitalized the consensus approach with his claims that early Americans did share a common set of anti-authoritarian values, and that the country was formed on the basis of these beliefs

NOTES

1   Bernard Bailyn, *The Ideological Origins of the American Revolution* (Cambridge, MA: Belknap Press, 1992), x.

2   Bailyn, *Ideological Origins*, xii.

THE PROBLEM

KEY POINTS

- At the time of the publication of *Ideological Origins*, historians of early America sought to uncover the causes of the American Revolution.*

- Historians who followed the lead of Charles Beard* explained that the American Revolution was the result of economic class conflict.

- While Bailyn emphasized the importance of ideas as the motor behind the American Revolution, he also developed a new understanding of the Revolution's intellectual origins.

Core Question

The core question that Bernard Bailyn tackles in *The Ideological Origins of the American Revolution* is: "What caused the American Revolution?" Bailyn refuted the common belief that the Revolution was driven by conflict between social groups, both between colonists and the British government and between different layers of American society. Instead he argued that the Revolution was driven by a conflict of political and ideological ideas.

Earlier scholarship had stressed American belief in the political theory of English political theorist John Locke.* Locke was a key figure in the Enlightenment* movement—an eighteenth-century European intellectual movement, promoting science and reason over tradition and religion. He argued that all people were born with inalienable—unchallengeable—rights, including life and liberty. He also taught that sovereignty (ultimate power) should be held by the

> **❝** Efforts to release Locke's hammerlock on the American mind were prominent in the argumentative strategies through which the republicanism project took shape. Bailyn, while not denying Locke's influence in eighteenth-century America, surrounded him with so large a mass of rival publicists and pamphleteers that his singularity disappeared. **❞**
>
> Daniel T. Rodgers, "Republicanism: The Career of a Concept"

people, not politicians, and that in an ideal democracy, the population accepts a "social contract" according to which individuals agree to grant legitimacy to a government, which in return serves the people and protects their rights.

While Bailyn agreed that Locke's philosophical views had influenced how Americans thought about the nature of government, he also identified an intellectual tradition stretching back to the English Civil War* of 1642 to 1651, which was fought between supporters of King Charles I and the institution of Parliament. This intellectual tradition was emphatic in its embrace of individual liberty and deeply suspicious of state authority. Bailyn wrote that such a fundamental anti-authoritarian strand of thought had conditioned the perceptions of the wider American public, and not just politicians and the educated elite. This streak of mistrust and suspicion radicalized the public's reaction to events such as the Stamp Act* crisis, when the British government attempted to increase tax revenue from the American colonies in 1765 by introducing tighter regulation of colonial trade. Suspicious colonists, however, interpreted the move as part of a broader conspiracy to restrict their political and economic freedom.

Bailyn argues that this perception would ultimately drive the colonies to seek independence.

The Participants

At the time of the publication of Bailyn's *Ideological Origins*, scholarship on the Revolution broke into two key camps. Those who followed the work of the progressive historian Charles Beard emphasized social conflict as the trigger for revolution; those who stressed the role of ideas included the political scientist Louis Hartz,* whose study of the intellectual origins of the Revolution asserted the impact of John Locke's thinking on American revolutionaries. A new generation of historians was, however, increasingly skeptical of this approach: Edmund S. Morgan,* for instance, sought to marginalize the importance of Locke's philosophies by highlighting the sheer diversity of revolutionary ideas at the time. Many of these ideas reflected a revolutionary radicalism and a paranoia about concentrated power.

As we have seen, Bailyn drew from the seemingly unrelated field of the history of the English Civil War to explain this paranoia—what he described as a "peculiar strain of anti-authoritarianism"[1] perpetually fearful of the power of ministerial conspiracy to undermine political freedoms—and so address this key problem in the existing research. This approach, while familiar to those working on the subject in British history, was highly original to American historians.

The Contemporary Debate

In his classic 1959 article "The Cult of the American Consensus: Homogenizing Our History," the American historian John Higham* lamented the decline of the social-conflict approach in the study of American history; he described the decline of the role of the analysis of social class and Marxist* thought in the study of American history (Marxism being an analytical movement following the political philosopher Karl Marx,* who saw class relations and conflict as the driving force of history). Higham also described the emergence of "a massive grading operation to smooth over America's social convulsions."[2] Bailyn can be seen as part of this generation of "homogenizers" (that is, standardizers), rejecting class warfare as the driving force of revolution, and instead emphasizing a shared set of republican and anti-authoritarian values that formed the basis of the United States.

More recent research has also highlighted a difficulty in *Ideological Origins*: how genuine was the pamphlets' rhetoric? Were the warnings that the British government was plotting to steal the colonists' freedoms really the expression of genuine thoughts and fears? Or were the pamphlets produced simply to support preexisting goals and desires that stemmed from economic or social conflicts?

Lastly, scholarship on early American life has moved its focus away from New England, which has affected the relevance of Bailyn's work. Critics argue that because most of the pamphlets originated from the urban northeast, Bailyn underestimated the range of economic, social, and political divisions and conflicts across the 13 British colonies that founded the United States. This criticism is leveled at much of the literature on early America from the 1950s and 1960s, in which an overemphasis on New England is said to have overly homogenized our picture of early America. However, despite these various issues, Bailyn's text remains influential and relevant to this day.

NOTES

1 Bernard Bailyn, *The Ideological Origins of the American Revolution* (Cambridge, MA: Belknap Press, 1992), xii.

2 John Higham, "The Cult of the 'American Consensus': Homogenizing Our History," *Commentary* 27 (1959): 93–100.

THE AUTHOR'S CONTRIBUTION

KEY POINTS

- Bailyn argued that the outbreak of the American Revolution* was due more to ideology than to class conflict.

- In making his argument, Bailyn challenged the dominant influence of Charles Beard* on the understanding of early American history.

- Bailyn's undertaking was in part a continuation of the work of the political scientist Louis Hartz,* who had demonstrated the influence of liberal English thinkers on leaders of the American Revolution.

Author's Aims

Bernard Bailyn's chief goal in writing *The Ideological Origins of the American Revolution* was to advance a groundbreaking new argument about the cause of the American Revolution. To this end, he sets out his argument in a coherent and well-researched manner. First, he presents his explanation for the Revolution's cause: a set of ideas that, when faced with the political developments from 1763 onward, caused colonists to perceive an immediate threat to their way of life and to their very liberty, which could be defended only with revolutionary violence.

Bailyn's next goal was to disarm the rival explanation, then dominant, that the Revolution was the result of simmering class or social conflict; he includes evidence to suggest that life in the colonies was broadly peaceful, and not riven with the inequality or tension that plagued eighteenth-century Europe. Bailyn's thorough history of

> ❝ Not since Charles Beard published his *Economic Interpretation of the Constitution* in 1913 has a single book so radically transformed the writing of American history. But where Beard's interpretive punch masked research that was both hasty and flawed, Bailyn's *Ideological Origins* has sources of power that will preserve its authority well into the new century. ❞
>
> Jack N. Rakove, "Encountering Bernard Bailyn"

colonists' revolutionary ideas, his reconstruction of the political events leading to the Revolution, and his argument about the nature of colonial society are all organized to provide an in-depth explanation of the American Revolution. Ultimately Bailyn realized this goal. He provides an account of the Revolution that also serves as a powerful critique of the rival social conflict* account.

Although Bailyn's argument would eventually be superseded, the broad strokes of his explanation remain persuasive and influential.

Approach

Bernard Bailyn arrived at the key concept of *Ideological Origins* by reading more than 400 political pamphlets produced during the period immediately prior to the American Revolution. Generally cheaply printed and short, they provide a valuable source of insight into the colonists' thinking. Many were written by future revolutionary leaders such as Reverend Jonathan Mayhew,* who coined the phrase "No taxation without representation"; similarly, the Massachusetts lawyer James Otis wrote: "Taxation without representation is tyranny." Both were protesting that the colonies were taxed by—but not represented within—the British government. As Bailyn explains, the pamphlets "reveal not merely positions taken but the reasons why positions were taken; they reveal motive and understanding: the assumptions, beliefs, and ideas—the articulated world view—that lay behind the manifest events of the time."[1]

Having read the pamphlets, and published an edited selection, Bailyn concluded that the colonists' revolutionary thought did not primarily originate in the ideas of the English political philosopher John Locke* or the rational, liberal* ideas of Enlightenment* thinkers, as many of Bailyn's contemporaries believed. Bailyn reached another conclusion—that the Revolution was rooted in a "peculiar strain of anti-authoritarianism bred in the upheaval of the English Civil War.*"[2] Although little attention had been paid to the opinions of these anti-authoritarians in eighteenth-century England, their ideas traveled to America and resonated with colonists.

Bailyn found that the revolutionary-era pamphlets contained an idealization of certain key ideals—the same ideals promoted by the English Civil War political rebels. In particular, these were the ideals of equality and popular sovereignty (where the population holds ultimate power, and is governed by consent). As the American pamphlets sought to interpret and explain their contemporary situation in the 13 colonies that would found the United States, they referenced the struggles of the English Levellers* (a political movement during the English Civil War that emphasized republican* ideals of popular sovereignty and equality). Bailyn believed these arguments were key to the Revolution that followed when the British government attempted to raise taxation on the colonies during the 1760s and 1770s. The suspicious colonists perceived a "deliberate assault launched surreptitiously by plotters against liberty both in England and in America."[3] This led to the Revolution, which Bailyn interpreted as an attempt to protect their existing liberty and society.

Contribution in Context

Bernard Bailyn's key concept in *Ideological Origins* was drawn from existing academic trends. Until then, the dominant narrative of the

American Revolution was associated with the influential political scientist Louis Hartz. Hartz argued that the political philosopher John Locke and the British liberalism movement were central to the colonists' political thinking (liberalism stresses the importance of individual freedom within politics). Yet Hartz did not acknowledge a certain radicalism that was evident to Bailyn in the period immediately prior to the Revolution. Similarly, Hartz failed to detect a kind of anxiety among the colonists about British political actions at that time.

Although Bailyn rejected many of Hartz's conclusions, Hartz's work remained influential to him in two key ways.

First, Bailyn agreed with Hartz that the Revolution was the result of ideological changes rather than being due to social conflicts, as earlier scholars such as Charles Beard had claimed. Second, Bailyn emphasized the importance of transatlantic connections between English and American thinkers in explaining revolutionary ideology. This echoed Hartz, who had highlighted the importation of Locke's ideas into the colonial context.

Furthermore, by including the ideas of both common people and politicians, Bailyn was democratizing intellectual history* by broadening the range of concepts seen to have influenced revolutionary ideology. This fits with two emerging trends among contemporary historians, who are moving past political histories that focus solely on political leaders, and beyond intellectual histories that focus on the Enlightenment philosophers.

NOTES

1   Bernard Bailyn, *The Ideological Origins of the American Revolution* (Cambridge, MA: Belknap Press, 1992), x.

2   Bailyn, *Ideological Origins*, xii.

3   Bailyn, *Ideological Origins*, 95.

SECTION 2
IDEAS

MAIN IDEAS

KEY POINTS

- The key theme of *Ideological Origins* is the radical political ideology that influenced the way in which American colonists perceived the actions of Britain toward their colony.

- Bailyn argued that the American Revolution* was, above all, founded on struggles over ideology and politics.

- He sought to demonstrate how the radical ideas developed by English anti-authoritarians during the English Civil War* a century earlier were adopted by American colonists to justify their independence from the British Empire.

Key Themes

In his attempt to explain the American Revolution, Bernard Bailyn presents four main themes in *The Ideological Origins of the American Revolution*. The first two—the radical political origins of revolutionary thought, and the ways in which anti-authoritarian ideas conditioned the colonists' perceptions of British politics, sparking revolutionary unrest—are closely related. These two themes interact to explain Bailyn's third great theme: the idea that the American Revolution was about preserving what the colonists perceived to be the existing social order, rather than radically remaking society. The fourth central theme of Bailyn's work concerns the ways in which ideas can condition people's perceptions of political events.

This provides Bailyn with the crucial link between revolutionary thought and action, helping explain how he arrives at what he

> **❝** The primary goal of the American Revolution which transferred American life and introduced a new era in human history, was not the overthrow or even the alteration of the existing social order but the preservation of political liberty threatened by the apparent corruption of the constitution, and the establishment in principle of the existing conditions of liberty. **❞**
>
> Bernard Bailyn, *The Ideological Origins of the American Revolution*

describes as his "rather old-fashioned view that the American Revolution was above all else an ideological, constitutional, [and] political struggle."[1]

Bailyn explains in the fourth chapter of *Ideological Origins* that "it is the meaning imparted to the events after 1763 by the integrated group of attitudes and ideas that lies behind the colonists' rebellion."[2] He argues that "the primary goal of the American Revolution … was not the overthrow or even the alteration of the existing social order but the preservation of political liberty threatened by the apparent corruption of the Constitution, and the establishment in principle of the existing conditions of liberty."

Exploring the Ideas

In *Ideological Origins*, Bailyn sets out to show that the central cause of the American Revolution was a particular intellectual current that conditioned colonists' perceptions of British policy during the 1760s and early 1770s, leading them to conclude that their way of life was under imminent threat. Bailyn builds his argument sequentially, and starts by reconstructing the revolutionary ideas about government formed by the period's intellectual climate. He begins with an examination of the colonists' mindset. Traditional intellectual histories of the Revolution had focused on how its political philosophy had been informed by the ideas of the English political philosopher John Locke.*

However, Bailyn's examination of revolutionary-era pamphlets suggests that a set of conspiratorially minded—and much more radical—thinkers was influential. Popular during the English Civil War* a century earlier, these anti-authoritarian thinkers had become marginal in England, although they remained prominent in the colonies. They argued that the central virtue of their society— liberty—was perpetually under threat from corrupt and power- hungry officials. In the fourth chapter of *Ideological Origins*, "The Logic of Rebellion," Bailyn argues that such ideas and attitudes became integrated into colonial thinking. These ideas then imparted meaning to the Stamp Act* crisis (the imposition by the British government of a direct tax on printed documents, including legal documents and newspapers, which provoked revolutionary feeling) and other events after 1763. For Bailyn, due to their particular interpretation of events, which could have been perceived very differently in an alternative intellectual climate, the colonists concluded that revolutionary action was necessary to protect their freedoms.

Language and Expression

Bailyn's work provides both a theoretical framework and a practical presentation, making it extremely persuasive. A number of criticisms of the text have emerged, mostly concerning the way in which Bailyn homogenizes (that is, standardizes) revolutionary ideas, neglecting the sheer diversity of positions taken by American colonists, and downplays colonial class conflict as a result of his emphasis on New England* and his neglect of the Chesapeake* and southern colonies. Contemporary studies have also paid more attention to class, race, and gender in early America. Bailyn's text nevertheless remains a key work on the Revolution. *Ideological Origins* is an extremely effective example of the ideas approach to understanding the American Revolution.

Similarly, his work serves as an excellent framework for understanding moments of historical change that can be used in a variety of contexts. It is a supreme example of a persuasive intellectual history* that clearly connects to historical events. Bailyn's explanation of the American Revolution allows readers to understand the colonists' motivations while also providing a framework for like-minded scholars to understand the relationship between ideas and historical events. As a result, its exemplary status is unlikely to be superseded any time soon, even if some of its content has been criticized.

NOTES

1   Bernard Bailyn, *The Ideological Origins of the American Revolution* (Cambridge, MA: Belknap Press, 1992), 94.

2   Bailyn, *Ideological Origins*, 51.

MODULE 6
SECONDARY IDEAS

KEY POINTS

- A key secondary idea of *Ideological Origins* was the flow of ideas and texts between England and the United States.

- Bailyn also highlighted the importance of conspiracy theories in unleashing the American Revolution,* and the relationship between revolutionary ideas and the Constitution* —the document setting out the obligations, limits, laws, and character of the government of the United States.

- Bailyn's attention to the impact of English radical ideas in early America helped launch the field of Atlantic history.*

Other Ideas

Beyond the core themes that Bernard Bailyn emphasizes in *The Ideological Origins of the American Revolution*, he develops a number of lesser but related topics. The key subsidiary ideas are the importance of the transatlantic flow of ideas (further developed in his late-career emphasis on Atlantic history) and the relationship between revolutionary ideology and the US Constitution, a link developed in a more recent edition of the book.

According to Bailyn, fear of high-level conspiracy was a key part of the revolutionary mindset. In *Ideological Origins*, he moves beyond the intellectual historians'* traditional emphasis on the more philosophical and highbrow ideas of John Locke* and the Enlightenment* as being key to the ideology of the Revolution. Bailyn instead reveals a previously undiscovered strain of anti-authoritarian thinking in the colonies that had originated from the English Civil War* and traveled to America

> ❝ Were the American Revolutionaries mentally disturbed? Was the Revolution itself a consequence of anxieties buried deep in the psyches of its leaders? Bizarre and preposterous questions, it would seem, and scarcely the sorts of questions one expects to be asked about the Founding Fathers. ❞
>
> Gordon S. Wood, "Conspiracy and the Paranoid Style: Causality and Deceit in the Eighteenth Century"

with the settlers. This manifested itself in the colonies as a deep suspicion of government and a belief that the British authorities were secretly plotting against the freedom of the colonists. As Bailyn observes in the chapter "A Note on Conspiracy," the colonists' belief in a pervasive conspiracy against their liberty "had deep and widespread roots that were elaborately embedded in Anglo-American political culture."[1]

Exploring the Ideas

The transatlantic approach to the flow of ideas proves enormously helpful for Bailyn's writing of *Ideological Origins*. His reconstruction of English radical politics during the eighteenth century builds on the work of scholars of English history. However, as it is common for scholarship to remain nationally focused (with, for example, English historians focusing on England), the relevance of these ideas in the American colonies has been underappreciated. By examining how texts circulate, Bailyn is able to introduce intellectual histories of England into the American context. Emphasizing the circulation of texts across national boundaries and across nations is enormously useful to academic historians. As such, it has become increasingly popular in the field of transnational history* (that is, a study of the movement of peoples, ideas, technologies, and institutions across national borders).

Later in his career, Bailyn deepened his interest in the cross-border circulation of texts. His popular Atlantic history seminar at Harvard promoted scholarship that examined the Atlantic rim* as a coherent historical unit. These studies sought to understand the flow of commodities, people, and ideas between the countries bordering the Atlantic Ocean—Europe, the coastal Americas, the Caribbean, and the African coast. A number of influential historians of early America, including Gordon Wood,* Jack Rakove,* and Michael Kammen, began their scholarly careers as participants in the Atlantic history seminar. It remains an important forum for the dissemination of scholarship on the history of the Atlantic World.

Overlooked

Because of the force of his argument and the importance of early America to public discourse, most aspects of Bernard Bailyn's *Ideological Origins* have been carefully scrutinized. Few areas of the text are neglected, and Bailyn's overall approach—the study of the relationship between ideas and the perception of political events—remains influential. Nevertheless, some aspects of the text are relatively overlooked, particularly Bailyn's emphasis on conspiracy. According to Bailyn, fear of conspiracy was a key part of the revolutionary mindset. In *Ideological Origins*, he introduced a radical yet popular school of thought, originally "bred in the upheaval of the English Civil War,"[2] which constantly feared conspiracy in government.

Scholars have since fully examined Bailyn's account of the colonists' understanding of legitimate government. Critics have also questioned the accuracy of Bailyn's claims that colonial life was relatively harmonious. However, the importance of conspiracy has been somewhat neglected, even though it comprises a major part of Bailyn's argument—and despite the fact that conspiracy has gone on to have a longer history in American politics. In the nineteenth century, fear of a conspiracy against slavery was at the core of the Southern secession that led to the American Civil War, and fear of slave conspiracies drove a great deal of violence during the Antebellum* years (the period between 1815 and the start of the Civil War in 1861). Even today, claims of conspiracy remain influential in American politics.

NOTES

1 Bernard Bailyn, *The Ideological Origins of the American Revolution* (Cambridge, MA: Belknap Press, 1992), 144.

2 Bailyn, *Ideological Origins,* xii.

MODULE 7
ACHIEVEMENT

KEY POINTS

- Bailyn's methodological approach to the study of the American Revolution* has become a model for historians studying revolutions in other periods and places.

- At the time of its publication, intellectual historians were increasingly attempting to connect political ideas to the concrete world of political action and mobilization.

- Bailyn's work did not consider the ideas and activities of socially marginal individuals in early American society.

Assessing the Argument

Bernard Bailyn's *The Ideological Origins of the American Revolution* has chiefly been influential in the discipline of history. However, as a wider public interest in the revolutionary period made Bailyn's work famous, the book has also had a broad impact outside the historical profession, for example with scholars of government and law. Because the United States' legal system operates on precedent (the idea that earlier rulings direct future rulings), there is an interest in the US Constitution*— the document setting out the laws, principles, and limits of the government of the United States—as a founding legal document. Although there is debate about how judges should engage with the Constitution, understanding the mindset of those who framed the Constitution is an important part of studying law.

As a result, many legal scholars are focused on the field of original intent*—researching the writings of those who framed the Constitution, with the belief that their original intentions while writing this key document need to be known, if today's political issues

> ❝ In *The Ideological Origins of the American Revolution,* the most famous of his works, Bailyn uncovered a set of ideas among the Revolutionary generation that most historians had scarcely known existed. These radical ideas about power and liberty, and deeply rooted fears of conspiracy, had propelled Americans in the 1760s and 1770s into the Revolution, Bailyn said. His book, which won the Pulitzer and Bancroft prizes in 1968, influenced an entire generation of historians. For many, it remains the most persuasive interpretation of the Revolution. ❞
>
> Gordon S. Wood, quoted in the *Wall Street Journal*

are to be resolved. As a result, scholars of original intent have engaged with historians such as Bailyn, as well as with historians Gordon Wood* and Jack Rakove,* both Pulitzer Prize* winners for their work on the Revolution and the Constitution. Because legal scholars and judges focus on ideology or "the intellectual climate" and textual interpretation when looking at the origins of laws or constitutions, they largely favor Bailyn's more ideological account of the American Revolution over explanations that emphasize social conflicts. Bailyn's work in *Ideological Origins* (as well as the work of Gordon Wood) has been important for lawyers and judges in helping them develop a fuller understanding of the Constitution's intellectual context.

Achievement in Context

Because Bailyn is making a historically specific argument in *Ideological Origins,* many of the ideas advanced in the book cannot be separated from their historical context. His broad approach to his subject still resonates with historians today, however, in that he moves beyond older political and intellectual histories and considers a broader range of sources. This means that *Ideological Origins* is not open to a common criticism often made by today's scholars regarding older histories: that historians of the past gave a disproportionate emphasis to the ideas and efforts of political leaders. Although some critics today might argue that Bailyn ignores the roles of the illiterate and socially marginal, he does still focus on a wide range of popular political pamphlets from a variety of cities and places.

Despite his argument being specific to a certain historical time, Bailyn's methodology is broadly effective for the study of a variety of literate cultures. Bailyn argues that "it is the meaning imparted to the events after 1763 by the integrated group of attitudes and ideas that lies behind the colonists' rebellion."[1] By emphasizing the ways in which ideas can influence the perception of events, he provides an effective example of how intellectual history* can be connected to mass action. This approach is as effective for the study of revolutionary America as it is for examinations of revolutionary France, twentieth-century China, and elsewhere.

Limitations

In *Forced Founders: Indians, Debtors, Slaves, and the Making of the American Revolution in Virginia* (1999) and its follow-up, *Unruly Americans and the Origins of the Constitution* (2007), the historian Woody Holton* provides a powerful argument for the importance of understanding social conflict.* In both books, Holton argues that socially marginal people—including the poor and slaves— were carrying out mass action and protest in the pre-Revolution years. This ultimately forced the colonial elites to pursue revolutionary action as a way to both quell the unrest and maintain their own power. Following Holton's narrative, the revolutionary ideology recorded by the elite (as in many of the pamphlets) is relevant only as an example of the justification made retroactively—that is, after the fact. Their writings were simply intended to validate the actions they had taken to maintain their own power in the face of mass protest.

This approach is an updated and highly nuanced version of the historian Charles Beard's* argument that the Constitution was about economic and political interests. Similarly, Holton's work has provided an effective critique of Bailyn's approach since, unlike Bailyn, Holton considers the Chesapeake* colonies (Maryland and Virginia), thus providing a fuller picture of American society at the time of the Revolution. This builds on earlier criticisms that Bailyn's picture of early America's intellectual landscape was too homogeneous. It seems, then, that historical approaches that focus on social conflict currently have the upper hand. It is nevertheless worth noting that these are often engaged in dialogue with intellectual histories. While Holton's approach is extremely persuasive, it is by no means the last word.

The other key shift in the historiography*—the historical scholarship—of the American Revolution is not a direct criticism of Bailyn but, rather, a sign that the kinds of questions that historians are considering about the Revolution have changed. In *The Marketplace of Revolution* (2005), the historian T. H. Breen,* professor of history emeritus at Northwestern University in Illinois, argues that historians must understand not just why the colonists took revolutionary action, but also *how* this kind of collective action was possible. According to Breen, consumer boycotts of British goods in response to British tax-raising measures provided the colonies with a framework for collective action. This united the disparate colonies through the shared experience of boycott. Breen argues that—independent of motivation—the American Revolution could not have occurred without such shared experience. This more recent research does not so much supersede *Ideological Origins* as decrease its relevance.

NOTES

1   Bernard Bailyn, *The Ideological Origins of the American Revolution* (Cambridge, MA: Belknap Press, 1992), 94.

PLACE IN THE AUTHOR'S WORK

KEY POINTS

- Bailyn's scholarship has focused primarily on the political culture of early America.

- Bailyn's *Ideological Origins* was an early work that helped establish him as a dominant figure in the historical scholarship of eighteenth-century America.

- *Ideological Origins* helped launch the field of Atlantic history,* examining the circulation of texts, ideas, commodities, and peoples around the Atlantic rim.*

Positioning

The Ideological Origins of the American Revolution, Bernard Bailyn's fourth book, represents a major contribution from a historian at the peak of his abilities. The book grew out of an introduction Bailyn wrote to an edited volume of key pamphlets from the revolutionary period, published in 1965 as *Pamphlets of the American Revolution, 1750–1776*. Ranging from a single sheet to dozens of pages in length, these pamphlets were widely circulated polemical* (provocative and controversial) tracts discussing the political events of the 1760s and 1770s. It was in the course of reading these pamphlets that Bailyn realized that the intellectual history of the Revolution was much deeper and more complicated than originally believed.

Bailyn's later work, notably *The New England Merchants in the Seventeenth Century*, would continue to explore the intellectual culture and economy of the American region of New England,* and was a natural outgrowth of his desire to understand early American identity and society. Bailyn would also continue to examine the intellectual

> ❝ For approximately half a century, Bailyn has been the country's most distinguished and influential scholar of the Revolution, the author of numerous books and the winner of prizes by the cartload. As professor of history at Harvard, he trained many of the younger scholars who have done so much to enhance our understanding of the period before, during and after the Revolution. It is no exaggeration to say that his influence on what the nation knows about its own beginnings is immense, if incalculable. ❞
>
> Jonathan Yardley, quoted in the *Washington Post*

and political origins of the American Revolution* further in subsequent books such as *The Ordeal of Thomas Hutchinson* (1974). Here, Bailyn studies the unfortunate fate of the royal governor of Massachusetts, whose mansion was ransacked due to his support of royal policy, and who was forced into exile in England, despite being born in the United States.

Integration

Bailyn's *Ideological Origins* helped establish him as a key figure in the discipline of Atlantic history, the historical subfield that studies the countries that border the Atlantic Ocean (that is, Europe, the coastal Americas, the Caribbean, and the African coast, known collectively as the Atlantic rim) as a coherent historical unit. It also studies the flow of commodities, people, and ideas between these lands. In subsequent works, notably *Voyagers to the West* (1986), Bailyn studied the process of transatlantic immigration and its far-reaching implications for human history.

Following the publication of *Ideological Origins*, Bailyn began organizing a seminar on Atlantic history at Harvard University that promoted Atlantic history scholarship by allowing scholars to present original research on the subject. While this emphasis on Atlantic history became much more self-conscious later in his career, the focus on transatlantic linkages was already a strong part of *Ideological Origins*.

As Bailyn explains: "I have sought to trace back into the early eighteenth century—and back into the European sources, wherever possible—the specific attitudes, conceptions, formulations, even in certain cases particular phrases, which together form the ideology of the American Revolution."[1] From his early work on the colonial economy to his revitalization of the intellectual history of the American Revolution, and his focus on Atlantic history in the 1990s and 2000s, Bailyn has had a major impact on the development of historical scholarship on the United States. Key to his impact has been Bailyn's coherent but constantly evolving body of work, as his interests have evolved along with the changing historical profession.

Significance

Ideological Origins has had far-reaching effects on scholarship on early America. Shortly after its publication, Bailyn was described as having "established a new paradigm for interpreting the Revolution" ("paradigm" refers to concepts or theories that provide a model for research within a field).[2] The work of Bailyn, his colleague J. G. A. Pocock,* and his former student Gordon Wood* became central to a new understanding of early American political thought. This new approach to early America was known as the Republican Synthesis* and it emphasized the philosophy of republicanism,* which the historian Robert Shalhope* explains is concerned with "maintaining public and private virtue, internal unity, social solidarity, and vigilance against the corruptions of power."[3]

Republican Synthesis remained popular for almost 20 years. More than a school of thought, it was widely used to explain the structure of the Constitution and the course of early American political history.

Although the Republican Synthesis approach remains important, it has lost some of its influence. As historians found republicanism everywhere in early America, it began to appear that any kind of political thought in early America could be deemed republican. The argument has certainly been made that, if republicanism can be found everywhere, the concept of Republican Synthesis is somewhat compromised; similarly, historians began to recognize that the meanings of frequently used core ideas in republicanism such as "virtue" were not all fixed, suggesting that the coherence in republican thought may have been more apparent than real.

NOTES

1   Bernard Bailyn, *The Ideological Origins of the American Revolution* (Cambridge, MA: Belknap Press, 1992), xvi.

2   Robert E. Shalhope, "Republicanism and Early American Historiography," *The William and Mary Quarterly* 39, no. 2 (1982): 335.

3   Shalhope, "Republicanism," 335.

SECTION 3
IMPACT

MODULE 9
THE FIRST RESPONSES

KEY POINTS

- Bailyn's work was criticized for overly standardizing early American political thought, for paying exclusive attention to the eastern region of New England,* and for ignoring social and economic divisions in early America.

- In succeeding editions of the work, Bailyn included analysis of a wider range of political pamphlets to prove the common intellectual foundations of political thought during the revolutionary period.

- Bailyn's work gave rise to a revisionist historiographical* movement— —a school of historical research that challenged orthodox interpretations—known as the Republican Synthesis.*

Criticism

In the immediate aftermath of its publication, Bernard Bailyn's *The Ideological Origins of the American Revolution* was criticized on two central grounds. First, Bailyn's reconstruction of revolutionary ideology was deemed inaccurate; second, his emphasis on ideas as opposed to social conflict* was thought to be problematic. While both critiques pose important challenges for Bailyn's account, they do not undermine his central explanation of the origins of revolutionary ideology.

The criticism of Bailyn's emphasis on ideas came from supporters of Marxist* and progressive* analyses of the American Revolution*— two approaches that highlighted the importance of social conflict in the Revolution. They began with historian Charles Beard's* 1913 book *An Economic Interpretation of the Constitution.* Beard argued that

> **"** J. G. A. Pocock, the third in the trinity of the
> 'republican synthesis,' had much to do with Wood's
> move away from Bailyn. Pocock's work stands in
> ambiguous temporal relation to that of the other
> two. His major work, *The Machiavellian Moment*,
> appeared after and drew from theirs, yet several
> shorter preliminary studies had appeared before Bailyn
> and Wood wrote and both scholars were obviously
> influenced by at least one of these earlier studies. Some
> of the difference between Bailyn and Wood stems from
> the greater degree to which Wood allowed Pocock's
> conceptions to shape him. **"**
>
> Michael P. Zuckert, *Natural Rights and the New Republicanism*

the Constitution,* more than being about political philosophy, was about advancing the interests of those who framed it. Supporters of Beard extended this self-interest argument to the wider revolutionary period, radically disputing the idea that the Revolution and Constitution were driven by high-minded abstract principles such as protecting liberty or freedom. According to this critical scholarship, which started in the 1970s, Bailyn provided an overly homogeneous view of early America by underestimating economic, social, and political divisions and conflicts in the colonies. This critique is leveled at much of the literature on early America written in the 1950s and 1960s, however, where an overemphasis on New England is said to distort our picture of early America.

Rather than undermining Bailyn's argument, these criticisms served to enrich his account, by inviting scholars to consider its relationship to other factors driving revolutionary politics. Bailyn himself addressed these concerns in later editions of the book by adding a postscript on the Constitution that explored the continuity between the document's framing and contemporary revolutionary rhetoric* (claims intended to influence or persuade people, often using dishonesty or exaggeration). This postscript represented an attempt to appease some of Beard's followers, who agreed that the American Revolution sought to overturn the traditional order but argued that the framing of the Constitution was a conservative move to promote stability for the elite.

In his discussion of the Constitution, Bailyn responded by suggesting that revolutionary rhetoric had never been about changing social structure. Instead, it was concerned with creating a new foundation for political authority, and the Constitution was a reflection of this desire.

Responses

The initial response to Bailyn's account of the American Revolution was extremely positive. While some people were somewhat critical of his intellectual approach, there were no criticisms that merited substantial modification. It would be some time before more powerful critiques would gain traction. The most persuasive criticism, that Bailyn over-standardized American intellectual life and over-emphasized New England by mostly focusing on pamphlets produced and circulated there, is one that was not made until well after the book's publication. Bailyn did make one change between the first version of his argument (presented as the introduction to *Pamphlets of the American Revolution*) and the version presented in *Ideological Origins*. This was an expansion of the breadth of pamphlets consulted, made so that he might claim a broader perspective on revolutionary intellectual life.

Some historians argued that Bailyn was too accepting of colonial rhetoric as genuine belief (although others did not see this as a major fault). In this reading, the era's conspiracy claims were merely a mode of expression, and did not actually represent a genuine fear of secret plotting. Bailyn's use of revolutionary sources in *Ideological Origins* was intended to answer this criticism; in these pamphlets he found a wide variety of modes of expression with common intellectual foundations. This suggested that he had reached insight into the Revolution that went beyond a mere analysis of rhetoric.

Some critics, among them Bailyn's former student Gordon Wood,* claimed that there was a break between the ideology of the American Revolution and the political thought of the period following independence. In his postscript on the Constitution, added to the twenty-fifth anniversary edition of *Ideological Origins*, Bailyn argued that there was, in fact, a continuity of ideas. On this point, he was clearly addressing Wood and his other critics. Although it is unclear which approach eventually gained the upper hand, in some sense both perspectives are correct. Bailyn agreed that revolutionary ideology did change somewhat in the Constitution; what was in dispute was merely how much, and where to draw the line.

Conflict and Consensus

Other criticisms came from scholars who broadly agreed with Bailyn's emphasis on ideology but who found ideas arising from different sources. J. G. A. Pocock, for example, traced revolutionary ideas about government and authority back to Italy during the Renaissance* (a period of intellectual and cultural history between the fourteenth and sixteenth centuries in which practitioners of the arts and architecture turned to classical Rome and Greece to reinvigorate European cultural forms), and to Niccolo Machiavelli,* a Florentine political thinker and author. Others argue that Bailyn oversimplified the diversity of political ideas in sixteenth- and seventeenth-century England to validate his argument. Yet other scholars observed that Bailyn focuses on a particularly narrow domain of political thought to explain the Revolution, ignoring many other cultural and intellectual realms, including religion.

As many historians, including Daniel Rodgers,* have observed, Bailyn was crucial in the creation of a consensus that placed republican* thought at the core of revolutionary and early national ideology—even though Bailyn himself never used the word "republican." However, his rejection of the political scientist John Locke* as the Revolution's key intellectual inspiration, his identification of multiple ideas (rather than just one) behind the Revolution, and his reinvigoration of intellectual approaches to the Revolution all provoked the search for a new framework of understanding. This culminated in what would become known as the Republican Synthesis—a movement in historical scholarship that emphasized republican thinking in early American political thought. Although muddied by conspiracy fears and beliefs about the need for independence, republicanism was at heart a set of ideas that held that good government was about "maintaining public and private virtue, internal unity, social solidarity, and vigilance against the corruptions of power."[1] Historian Robert Shalhope* states that Bailyn was the "progenitor of this new appreciation of Republicanism,"[2] and Bailyn's approach remained dominant for decades after the publication of *Ideological Origins*.

NOTES

1   Robert E. Shalhope, "Republicanism and Early American Historiography," *The William and Mary Quarterly* 39, no. 2 (1982): 335.

2   Shalhope, "Republicanism," 334.

MODULE 10
THE EVOLVING DEBATE

KEY POINTS

- Bailyn's *Ideological Origins* undermined the importance of the English political philosopher John Locke* in the intellectual history* of early America.

- The Republican Synthesis* emerged as a dominant conceptual model in early American history following the publication of *Ideological Origins*.

- Largely shaped by Bailyn himself, the field of Atlantic history* developed in the years following the publication of *Ideological Origins*.

Uses and Problems

While Bernard Bailyn has few self-professed intellectual "disciples," he has had a long career as an advisor at Harvard University, and his Atlantic history seminar has trained many influential historians. One of his former students, Gordon Wood,* is now one of the best-known historians of early America. Wood has won the Pulitzer Prize,* as have Michael Kammen* and Jack Rakove,* two more of Bailyn's former students. All three have produced significant work on the American Revolution,* much of it engaging directly with Bailyn's work.

Gordon Wood examines the history of American political thought in *The Creation of the American Republic, 1776–1787* (1969). Although he broadly accepts Bailyn's ideas about the origins of the American Revolution, he extends Bailyn's argument by arguing that the Constitution* of the United States represented a break from revolutionary ideology. Wood claims that during their first years of

> **❝**How this came about, the emergence of this interest in Atlantic history as more than a geographical expression—as a subject itself, as a historical conception, as an essential passage in the development of the world we know—has its own history. It is a story that winds through the public life of the late twentieth century, through the interior impulses of technical scholarship, and through the social situation of those who write history. **❞**
>
> Bernard Bailyn, *Atlantic History: Concept and Contours*

independence, Americans recognized that their old society could not be recreated, and that ongoing social conflict* would have to be managed. Similarly, Jack Rakove's 1996 book *Original Meanings: Politics and Ideas in the Making of the Constitution* shares Bailyn's interest in early American political thought. But in examining the idea of original intent*—understanding the intentions of those who framed the Constitution in order to address current political issues— Rakove extends Bailyn's scholarship by exploring how the study of early America has implications for the present day. Both books illustrate how Bailyn's students critically engaged with his work.

Bailyn has had most influence through his Atlantic history annual seminars, which Rakove has described as a "transforming intellectual experience."[1] According to organizers, the seminars have supported more than 300 historians from hundreds of institutions worldwide and have provided crucial support for many influential historians at early stages of their careers, including the Atlantic historian David Armitage,* the western historian Ned Blackhawk,* and others. They also inspired much of Bailyn's own work; he dedicated his 2005 book *Atlantic History: Concepts and Contours* to the seminars.

Schools of Thought

Bailyn's *Ideological Origins* had two sizable effects on academic readings of early American history. First, it undermined the focus on John Locke and his political thought in shaping the ideas of the revolutionaries. Second, it supported the rise of the Republican Synthesis movement, with its focus on republicanism.* While Bailyn did not entirely reject readings of history that looked to Locke's ideas, he introduced new strains from radical and anti-authoritarian English thought. These emphasized liberty, fear of centralized power, and concerns about a pervasive conspiracy against colonial freedom.

Bailyn explained that, for the colonists, "fear of a comprehensive conspiracy against liberty throughout the English-speaking world—a conspiracy believed to have been nourished in corruption, and of which, it was felt, oppression in America was only the most immediately visible part—lay at the heart of the revolutionary movement."[2] Around this belief, Bailyn, his colleague J. G. A. Pocock,* and his former student Gordon Wood founded a set of ideas that became central to a new understanding of early American political thought. This emphasized republicanism, a political philosophy concerned with "maintaining public and private virtue, internal unity, social solidarity, and vigilance against the corruptions of power," as explained by Robert Shalhope.*[3]

This new approach, named the Republican Synthesis, was popular for almost 20 years and was used to explain the structure of the Constitution and early American political history. Although this paradigm was fundamentally questioned as historians working in several fields began identifying republicanism in other historical contexts, the specifics of Bailyn's approach still remain influential.

In Current Scholarship

Bailyn's emphasis on Atlantic history has endured. Central to his argument in *Ideological Origins* is the transatlantic flow of political ideas from England to the colonies, decisive in shaping the colonial mindset. This flow had previously been ignored by historians, but Bailyn proved its influence convincingly. As historians began considering interactions across the Atlantic for the first time, the field became known as Atlantic history. Thanks to Bailyn's Atlantic history seminars at Harvard University, it became an identifiable school of thought examining the flow of people, ideas, and goods between the countries around the Atlantic rim.* *Ideological Origins* has thus inspired a variety of scholars in the fields of American and Atlantic history. While many of these scholars have grappled with and criticized Bailyn's approach, the influence of his text remains.

Another important change in the intellectual environment has been a shift in focus from simply considering the causes of the American Revolution or the origins of American political thought toward what made the Revolution possible, or how different colonies came to see a common cause. Rather than presupposing social unity among the colonies, which Bailyn sometimes appears to do, this more recent scholarship tries to understand how the colonies united. T. H. Breen's* *The Marketplace of Revolution* (2005) is perhaps the best example, examining how consumer boycotts against British goods not only constituted political action but later helped the various colonies to coordinate their efforts against such British measures as the Stamp Act* (a controversial piece of legislation passed to impose a direct tax on printed documents).

Ideological Origins has had two long-term impacts. First, the book led to the emergence of the Republican Synthesis, which became the dominant understanding of the Revolution for decades. While this movement has been somewhat overturned, it still remains influential. Second, Bailyn's account revitalized the field of intellectual histories of the American Revolution and early republic. Although this approach remains under attack from conflict-centered accounts, it nonetheless remains a key aspect of the ongoing debate.

Despite the fact that there have been dramatic changes to the field of early American history since the 1960s, when *Ideological Origins* was published, Bailyn's book remains central to much scholarly study and debate.

NOTES

1   Jack Rakove, "Encountering Bernard Bailyn: An Appreciation," *Humanities* 19, no. 2 (1998).

2   Bernard Bailyn, *The Ideological Origins of the American Revolution* (Cambridge, MA: Belknap Press, 1992), XIII.

3   Robert E. Shalhope, "Republicanism and Early American Historiography," *The William and Mary Quarterly* 39, no. 2 (1982): 335.

MODULE 11
IMPACT AND INFLUENCE TODAY

KEY POINTS

- Bailyn's *Ideological Origins* remains a reference point for intellectual histories* of the American Revolution.*

- A revival of social conflict*-centered approaches to the American Revolution (interpretations that consider the struggle between social classes, for example, to be central) have to a certain degree undermined the relevance of Bailyn's work for the historiography* (historical study) of early America.

- Recent work on the ideological origins of the American Revolution has shifted to colonies not studied by Bailyn, notably Virginia and Maryland.

Position

If Bernard Bailyn's *The Ideological Origins of the American Revolution* remains relevant despite the fact that newer accounts have superseded it, this is due in part to the artfulness with which it was constructed— it is the most impressive example of Bailyn's characteristically thorough approach. Even if significant parts of his argument are problematic, Bailyn has nevertheless provided a persuasive way of thinking about the Revolution, which other historians must still grapple with.

Two recent factors have, however, served to limit the book's relevance today. First, a reinvigoration of accounts of the Revolution's origins that emphasize social conflict;* second, a move away from looking for motivations for the Revolution toward examining how revolutionary action was possible.

> ❝ On one topic, however, Professor Bailyn and I agree:
> the need for further attention to native Americans and
> blacks. The essentially Eurocentric perspective that he
> adopts in these initial volumes makes it more difficult
> for the general reader to appreciate the complex and
> creative patterns of racial interaction that occurred
> throughout the colonies. ❞
>
> T. H. Breen to Bernard Bailyn, "Now, Voyager," in the *New York Review of Books*

Although Bailyn's argument has met with strong criticism, it retains a good deal of relevance to contemporary debates. His framework for understanding the Revolution by considering how ideas conditioned colonists' perceptions remains persuasive, even to those who emphasize social conflict. For example, the historian Woody Holton,* in his accounts of the Revolution, describes the mass unrest and protest of the socially marginalized, including the poor and slaves. He describes this social conflict as a key driver of the Revolution. However, these poorer colonists' perceptions of their place in society still affected their collective action—and some sort of ideological perspective still conditioned their perceptions. Similarly, any inquiry into how revolution was possible, as in the work of the revolutionary scholar T. H. Breen,* still has to consider the motives behind the uprising. *Ideological Origins* remains relevant both as an example of one perspective on historical change—emphasizing the force of ideas—and as a masterpiece of detailed and persuasive historical writing.

Interaction

The most recent pressure to be applied to Bailyn's account has come from new historical research that argues that the main driver for the

Revolution was the tension between different classes and social groups within the colonies. This highlights a key difficulty in Bailyn's account—the problem of how to determine whether the rhetoric* in the pamphlets was genuine. Were the warnings of conspiracies based on genuine thoughts and fears, or written to justify the plans of an elite whose revolutionary goals were in fact rooted in economic or social self-interest? Nevertheless, Bailyn's claim that certain ideas conditioned colonists' perceptions is powerful, even if the specific content of such thinking needs more analysis. As a key text in the constantly evolving field of early American history, *Ideological Origins* has been thoroughly critiqued since its publication, yet it remains highly influential in contemporary debates today.

While Bailyn challenged rival intellectual histories of the origins of the American Revolution, the key school to come under attack is the social-conflict explanation, rooted in the work of Charles Beard.* Although Beard's 1913 book *An Economic Interpretation of the Constitution of the United States* has now been superseded, accounts of the Revolution based on class interests remain influential. In 2005, the historian Gary Nash* wrote *The Unknown American Revolution: The Unruly Birth of Democracy and the Struggle to Create America*. This describes how a growing radicalism among the working classes in urban centers such as Boston produced a more active protest to British actions that had outraged colonists across America more generally. Nash claims this was a central factor in accounting for the Revolution. To him, the intellectual story was important, but class conflict drove the fighting with the British as much as abstract ideas. His argument is especially significant because he examines the same major northeastern cities in which the pamphlets studied by Bailyn had circulated.

Lastly, the focus away from New England* in scholarship on early America has somewhat affected the relevance of Bailyn's work. Critics argue that because of his emphasis on pamphlets from the urban northeast, Bailyn ignored or underestimated many economic, social, or political divisions of the time, and presented an overly uniform view of the settlers' ideas. However, this criticism can be leveled at most of the histories of early America written in the 1950s and early 1960s. Only with the emergence of New Left* history at the end of the 1960s would historians pay greater attention to class, race, and gender within early American society (the New Left was a political movement that sought a range of reforms concerning gay rights, gender roles, and the treatment of racial minorities).

The Continuing Debate

The debate over *Ideological Origins* remains active partly because it carries a strong political undercurrent, stretching right back to the conflict between progressive* and consensus* historians. Because consensus histories such as Bailyn's emphasize the negotiation of shared core "American values" in the formation of the country, as opposed to violent conflict over economic distribution or civil rights, they are generally optimistic about the United States and the American identity. In contrast, accounts that emphasize social conflict carry the political implication that the American identity is a result of struggles between marginal people and the elites who tried to exclude them.

The historian Woody Holton is one advocate of this conflict-based approach. In *Forced Founders: Indians, Debtors, Slaves, and the Making of the American Revolution in Virginia* (1999), he argues that the American Revolution was perpetuated by the white elites who hoped to mollify angry, socially marginal Americans—but only in order to advance their own interests. Holton's self-interest-based argument is a fairly direct critique of Bailyn's presentation of a unified society fighting to protect its liberty. However, the conflict-based approach is indeed more appropriate in the colonies around the Chesapeake Bay* that Holton examines. *Forced Founders* particularly focuses on Virginia, where Holton's account is persuasive. Yet Bailyn's approach remains accurate for areas such as New England, so all is not lost for his intellectual history perspective.

Because the revolutionary period is so central to American identity, the debate over the origins of the American Revolution remains current in both academic history and the popular realm. Academically, parts of the debate have moved from determining the Revolution's origins and causes to looking at how a successful revolutionary movement was possible. However, the work of Woody Holton, including his more recent *Unruly Americans and the Origins of the Constitution* (2007), shows that the debate over its origins remains current.

WHERE NEXT?

KEY POINTS

- Bailyn's work will likely continue to have a lasting influence on the historiography*—written historical scholarship—of the American Revolution.*

- Ideological Origins remains a seminal example of the new approach to intellectual history*—the study of ideas in history—that developed beginning in the 1960s.

- The text will continue to have the greatest impact on intellectual historians researching early America.

Potential

Bernard Bailyn's *The Ideological Origins of the American Revolution* looks set to remain influential in both the public and academic realms. This is because Bailyn's core argument—that a set of ideas that stretched back to the English Civil War* about power, the state, and freedom, colored the colonists' perception of British policy in the 1760s and ultimately sparked the American Revolution*—remains persuasive. Although academic historians have criticized some of the specifics of Bailyn's argument, his clear and persuasive writing means that the book will persist for students and scholars as both a model and as an example of powerful historical argument. Similarly, the general public will continue to have an ongoing interest in the Revolution, and Bailyn's work remains exemplary as a text that puts ideas at the heart of the Revolution.

In addition to the lasting power of Bailyn's argument, this book is likely to have a very long shelf life, in keeping with other works on early America. While *Ideological Origins* remains relevant more than 40 years after its original publication, this is a short span compared with

> **❝** With this reading of the American Revolutionary Experience, Mr. Bailyn has substantially and profoundly altered the nature and direction of the inquiry on the American Revolution. In the process he has also erected a new framework for interpreting the entire first half-century of American national history ... A landmark in American historiography. **❞**
>
> American Quarterly

Charles Beard's* *An Economic Interpretation of the Constitution of the United States*, published in 1913. The debate over the origins of the Constitution and American identity and politics remains relevant today, and if the ongoing significance of Beard's text is any indication, *Ideological Origins* will remain influential for decades to come.

Future Directions

Several of Bailyn's former students have extended the arguments developed in *Ideological Origins*. For example, Gordon Wood,* in *The Creation of the American Republic, 1776–1787* (1969), examines the history of American political thought, broadly accepting Bailyn's argument about the origins of the American Revolution while extending it by considering not only the Revolution's origins but its conclusion with the signing of the Constitution* in 1787. Wood argues that the Constitution represented a break from revolutionary ideology—following their independence from the British, Americans realized that they could not recreate their previous society, and that social conflict could not be eradicated, merely managed.

Similarly, Jack Rakove's* book *Original Meanings: Politics and Ideas in the Making of the Constitution* (1996) shares Bailyn's interest in early American political thought. But in examining the idea of original intent*—understanding the intentions of the framers of the

Constitution in order to address current political issues—Rakove extends Bailyn's scholarship by exploring the present-day implications of work on early America. These two books illustrate how Bailyn's students have critically engaged with his work.

Bailyn has had most influence through his annual Atlantic history* seminars. Most of the seminar participants are indirect disciples of Bailyn and his work. Although *Ideological Origins* was central to Bailyn's career, his longevity as a scholar means that his scholarly influence is greater than the impact of any one particular book. Nevertheless, many of his students and collaborators continue to advance the ideas developed in *Ideological Origins*, centering on his belief that the search for American identity is to be found in the revolutionary era.

Summary

In *The Ideological Origins of the American Revolution*, Bernard Bailyn sought to explain the causes of the American Revolution. In so doing, he hoped to answer an apparent paradox: while Bailyn believed the American Revolution to have been radical, he also observed that it was "not primarily a controversy between social groups undertaken to force changes in the organization of the society or the economy."[1] His explanation turns on his belief that the American Revolution was above all else driven by the colonists' ideas and beliefs about politics and the constitutions of nations. Bailyn reconstructs these ideas through a broad examination of popular political pamphlets that circulated in the United States and England throughout the eighteenth century. By doing this, he moves beyond the traditional emphasis on the more philosophical ideals of John Locke* and the Enlightenment* in explaining revolutionary ideology. Instead, Bailyn finds a strand of radical English thought suspicious of state power and that advocated violent resistance to protect individual liberty.

As the historian of American political culture Robert Shalhope* writes, Bailyn was the "progenitor of this new appreciation of

Republicanism";[2] his account became central to a newly accepted model for understanding early American history, known as the Republican Synthesis.* This approach holds that a set of republican ideas characterized early American political thought, that these ideas included a suspicion of British authority, and that political systems should be developed to check some of the central tensions that exist with any free political system. The argument remained dominant for several decades after the publication of *Ideological Origins*, and Bailyn's book received a Pulitzer Prize.* He also became a public intellectual, as *Ideological Origins* found a readership beyond the academic world. Bailyn went on to write many more influential books, including the Pulitzer Prize-winning *Voyagers to the West: A Passage in the Peopling of American on the Eve of the Revolution* (1986).[3]

Ideological Origins is set apart from other studies of the American Revolution, both because of the force of its argument at the time of its publication and because of the great skill with which it is written. Theoretically nuanced and rigorously objective in its research, Bailyn's book is an example of effective historical scholarship aimed at both teachers and students. With clear, forceful writing, Bailyn crafted a persuasive account of the American Revolution. Though criticisms over the past 40 years suggest his original account may need modification, the book retains a great deal of relevance and will likely remain part of the debate about the Revolution for many years to come.

NOTES

1   Bernard Bailyn, *The Ideological Origins of the American Revolution* (Cambridge, MA: Belknap Press, 1992), x.

2   Robert E. Shalhope, "Republicanism and Early American Historiography," *The William and Mary Quarterly* 39, no. 2 (1982): 334.

3   Bernard Bailyn, *Voyagers to the West: A Passage in the Peopling of America on the Eve of the Revolution* (New York: Knopf, 1986).

GLOSSARY

GLOSSARY OF TERMS

American Revolution: a war occurring between 1775 and 1783, waged against England by the 13 colonies that would eventually comprise the United States, in a bid to secure their independence.

Antebellum: in American history, generally considered to be the period between the War of 1812 and the American Civil War (1861–5.)

Atlantic history: a historical subfield that studies the Atlantic rim as a coherent historical unit, and examines the flow of commodities, people, and ideas between Europe, the coastal Americas, the Caribbean, and the African coast.

Atlantic rim: the countries that border the Atlantic Ocean.

Bancroft Prize: a prize awarded yearly by Columbia University to authors of books about American history or diplomatic history.

Capitalism: the economic and social model, dominant in the West and increasingly throughout the developing world, in which industry and resources are held in private hands.

Catholicism: also known as Roman Catholicism, a Christian religion that follows the teachings and structure of Christianity's classical origins. The Pope is the supreme authority of this religion.

Chesapeake colonies: the American colonies situated around the Chesapeake Bay—Maryland and Virginia.

Cold War: a period of intense political and economic rivalry that developed between the United States and the Soviet Union following World War II and which continued until the collapse of the Soviet Union in 1991.

Consensus history: a historiographical tradition that emphasizes the negotiation of shared core values (often surrounding ideas about freedom or liberty) rather than social conflict as the key driver of American history.

Constitution: a document that sets out the laws, obligations, and principles of a nation's government.

Constitutional: relating to the system of beliefs and laws that govern a country: of or relating to a constitution.

Continental Congress: the governing body for the original 13 American colonies during the revolutionary period. Its first meeting was held in 1774.

English Civil War: a series of conflicts between 1642 and 1651 fought by followers of King Charles I and supporters of Parliament, England's supreme legislative body.

Enlightenment: a far-ranging intellectual movement in eighteenth-century Europe, known for its emphasis on reason and human progress.

Great Awakening: an evangelical religious movement that swept through Protestant Europe and the American colonies in the 1730s and 1740s.

Historiography: the historical scholarship on a given subject.

Intellectual history: the study of ideas in history.

Levellers: a political movement during the English Civil War that emphasized republican ideals of popular sovereignty and equality.

Liberalism: a philosophy that puts the nature and extent of individual freedom at the center of political questions.

Marxism: a method of analysis, derived from the writings of the political philosopher Karl Marx, that sees class relations and class conflict as the driving force of history.

New England: a region that encompasses the present-day northeastern United States. In the colonial period, it spanned the Massachusetts Bay, Connecticut, Rhode Island and Providence Plantations, and New Hampshire colonies.

New Left: a political movement in the 1960s and 1970s that sought to implement a range of reforms concerning gay rights, gender roles, and the treatment of racial minorities. It was in contrast to the traditional Marxist left, which focused on class struggle and labor unionization.

Original intent: the belief that the intentions of those who framed the Constitution need to be understood in order to resolve today's political issues.

Paradigm: a set of concepts or theories that provides a model for research in a field.

Polemical: a controversial set of propositions that are meant to elicit debate and disputes.

Progressive historians: historians such as Charles Beard who emphasize the importance of conflict throughout American history.

Protestantism: one of the two principle branches of Christianity. Protestants reject many of the doctrines of the Catholic Church, notably the meaning of certain rituals and the status of the Catholic Pope.

Pulitzer Prize: a set of prizes awarded to authors of works in 21 categories that include work in journalism, literature, music, and general non-fiction.

Puritans: a group of English reformed Protestants in the sixteenth and seventeenth century, many of whom emigrated to the United States in the 1630s.

Renaissance Italy: a period of intellectual and cultural change in Italy between the fourteenth and sixteenth centuries.

Republicanism: the belief that the supreme power in any country should be held by the electorate, who create and oversee their government by common consent.

Republican Synthesis: a historical movement, led by Bernard Bailyn, his colleague J. G. A. Pocock, and his former student Gordon Wood, that emphasized republican thinking in early American political thought.

Rhetoric: language intended to influence or persuade people—often (but not exclusively) understood to employ figures of speech or exaggeration, which may not be honest or reasonable.

Social conflict: the struggle that occurs between different social groups for power.

Soviet Union: a former state comprising present-day Russia and parts of Eastern Europe and central Asia; it was the United States' chief rival during the Cold War.

Stamp Act of 1765: a measure intended to increase revenue from the American colonies. It was a direct tax on printed documents, including legal documents and newspapers. These documents had to be printed on specially produced paper bearing a revenue stamp.

Transnational history: the study of the historical movement of peoples, ideas, technologies, and institutions across different nations.

Williams College: a liberal arts college in western Massachusetts.

World War II (1939–45): a global war that pitted the Axis powers (chiefly Germany and Japan) against the Allied powers (chiefly the Soviet Union, Great Britain, the United States, and France).

PEOPLE MENTIONED IN THE TEXT

David Armitage (b. 1965) is a British historian, and professor of history at Harvard University, known for his work on intellectual and international history of the early modern era.

Charles Beard (1874–1948) was a historian at Columbia University and, later in his career, co-founder of the New School in New York City. He is best known for his books *An Economic Interpretation of the Constitution of the United States* (1913) and *The Rise of American Civilization* (1927).

Ned Blackhawk (b. 1970) is professor of western history at Yale University, best known for his work *Violence over the Land: Indians and Empires in the Early American West* (2006).

T. H. Breen (b. 1942) is a professor of history emeritus at Northwestern University in Illinois, and a specialist on the American Revolution.

Jonathan Edwards (1703–58) was a Puritan theologian and preacher known for his role in sparking the "Great Awakening" religious movement.

Oscar Handlin (1915–2011) was a professor of history at Harvard University, most notable for his work on immigration in the United States.

Louis Hartz (1919–86) was a political scientist best known for his book *The Liberal Tradition in America* (1955).

John Higham (1920–2003) was an American cultural historian who wrote on ethnicity and national identity.

Woody Holton is professor of history at the University of South Carolina, best known for his book *Forced Founders: Indians, Debtors, Slaves and the Making of the American Revolution* (1999).

Michael Kammen (1936–2013) was an American historian at Cornell University, who received the Pulitzer Prize in 1973 for his book *People of Paradox: An Inquiry Concerning the Origins of American Civilization* (1972).

John Locke (1632–1704) was an English philosopher and political theorist, influential in the Enlightenment movement. He argued that all men were born with inalienable rights to life and liberty. His 1689 work *Two Treatises of Government* examined the foundations of legitimate rule.

Niccolo Machiavelli (1469–1527) was a Florentine political thinker, best known for his 1513 treatise *The Prince*.

Karl Marx (1818–83) was a German philosopher, political theorist, and economist. Marx was the major historical theorist of communism, and his prodigious output includes *Das Kapital* (1867).

Jonathan Mayhew (1720–66) was an American minister famous for coining the phrase "No taxation without representation."

Perry Miller (1905–63) was an intellectual historian and professor at Harvard University known for his studies relating to the intellectual life of New England and its connection to American identity.

Edmund S. Morgan (1916–2013) was an American historian at Yale University from 1955 to 1986. He specialized in early American history.

Samuel Eliot Morison (1887–1976) was an American historian noted for his works on maritime history.

Gary Nash (b. 1933) is an American historian who specializes in the revolutionary period and slavery in early America.

James Otis (1725–83) was a lawyer in colonial Massachusetts, remembered for his phrase "Taxation without representation is tyranny."

J. G. A. Pocock (b. 1924) is professor emeritus at Johns Hopkins University, and a noted historian of political thought and republicanism in the early modern period.

Jack Rakove (b. 1947) is a historian at Stanford University, who received the 1996 Pulitzer Prize for his book *Original Meanings: Politics and Ideas in the Making of the Constitution*.

Daniel Rodgers (b. 1942) is emeritus professor of history at Princeton University, a specialist in American intellectual and cultural history.

Robert E. Shalhope (b. 1941) is a historian at the University of Oklahoma, who specializes in the history of American political culture between 1760 and 1876.

Gordon S. Wood (b. 1933) is professor of history emeritus at Brown University; he received the 1993 Pulitzer Prize for his book *The Radicalism of the American Revolution*.

WORKS CITED

WORKS CITED

Bailyn, Bernard. *Atlantic History: Concepts and Contours*. Cambridge, MA: Harvard University Press, 2005.

The Ideological Origins of the American Revolution. Cambridge, MA: Belknap Press, 1992.

Voyagers to the West: A Passage in the Peopling of America on the Eve of the Revolution. New York: Knopf, 1986.

Fink, Z. S. "Review of the Ideological Origins of the American Revolution." *Historical Journal* 11, no. 3 (1968): 588–90.

Higham, John. "The Cult of the 'American Consensus': Homogenizing Our History." *Commentary* 27 (1959): 93–100.

Rakove, Jack N. "Encountering Bernard Bailyn." *Humanities* 19, no. 2 (1998).

Rodgers, Daniel T. "Republicanism: The Career of a Concept." *The Journal of American History* 79, no. 1 (1992): 11–38.

Ross, Steven J. "The Transformation of Republican Ideology." *Journal of the Early Republic* 10, no. 3 (1990): 323–30.

Shalhope, Robert E. "Republicanism and Early American Historiography." *The William and Mary Quarterly* 39, no. 2 (1982): 334–56.

Wood, Gordon S. "Conspiracy and the Paranoid Style: Causality and Deceit in the Eighteenth Century." *The William and Mary Quarterly* 39, no. 3 (1982): 401–41

Zuckert, Michael P. *Natural Rights and the New Republicanism*. Princeton: Princeton University Press, 1994.

THE MACAT LIBRARY
BY DISCIPLINE

AFRICANA STUDIES

Chinua Achebe's *An Image of Africa: Racism in Conrad's Heart of Darkness*
W. E. B. Du Bois's *The Souls of Black Folk*
Zora Neale Huston's *Characteristics of Negro Expression*
Martin Luther King Jr's *Why We Can't Wait*
Toni Morrison's *Playing in the Dark: Whiteness in the American Literary Imagination*

ANTHROPOLOGY

Arjun Appadurai's *Modernity at Large: Cultural Dimensions of Globalisation*
Philippe Ariès's *Centuries of Childhood*
Franz Boas's *Race, Language and Culture*
Kim Chan & Renée Mauborgne's *Blue Ocean Strategy*
Jared Diamond's *Guns, Germs & Steel: the Fate of Human Societies*
Jared Diamond's *Collapse: How Societies Choose to Fail or Survive*
E. E. Evans-Pritchard's *Witchcraft, Oracles and Magic Among the Azande*
James Ferguson's *The Anti-Politics Machine*
Clifford Geertz's *The Interpretation of Cultures*
David Graeber's *Debt: the First 5000 Years*
Karen Ho's *Liquidated: An Ethnography of Wall Street*
Geert Hofstede's *Culture's Consequences: Comparing Values, Behaviors, Institutes and Organizations across Nations*
Claude Lévi-Strauss's *Structural Anthropology*
Jay Macleod's *Ain't No Makin' It: Aspirations and Attainment in a Low-Income Neighborhood*
Saba Mahmood's *The Politics of Piety: The Islamic Revival and the Feminist Subjec*t
Marcel Mauss's *The Gift*

BUSINESS

Jean Lave & Etienne Wenger's *Situated Learning*
Theodore Levitt's *Marketing Myopia*
Burton G. Malkiel's *A Random Walk Down Wall Street*
Douglas McGregor's *The Human Side of Enterprise*
Michael Porter's *Competitive Strategy: Creating and Sustaining Superior Performance*
John Kotter's *Leading Change*
C. K. Prahalad & Gary Hamel's *The Core Competence of the Corporation*

CRIMINOLOGY

Michelle Alexander's *The New Jim Crow: Mass Incarceration in the Age of Colorblindness*
Michael R. Gottfredson & Travis Hirschi's *A General Theory of Crime*
Richard Herrnstein & Charles A. Murray's *The Bell Curve: Intelligence and Class Structure in American Life*
Elizabeth Loftus's *Eyewitness Testimony*
Jay Macleod's *Ain't No Makin' It: Aspirations and Attainment in a Low-Income Neighborhood*
Philip Zimbardo's *The Lucifer Effect*

ECONOMICS

Janet Abu-Lughod's *Before European Hegemony*
Ha-Joon Chang's *Kicking Away the Ladder*
David Brion Davis's *The Problem of Slavery in the Age of Revolution*
Milton Friedman's *The Role of Monetary Policy*
Milton Friedman's *Capitalism and Freedom*
David Graeber's *Debt: the First 5000 Years*
Friedrich Hayek's *The Road to Serfdom*
Karen Ho's *Liquidated: An Ethnography of Wall Street*

John Maynard Keynes's *The General Theory of Employment, Interest and Money*
Charles P. Kindleberger's *Manias, Panics and Crashes*
Robert Lucas's *Why Doesn't Capital Flow from Rich to Poor Countries?*
Burton G. Malkiel's *A Random Walk Down Wall Street*
Thomas Robert Malthus's *An Essay on the Principle of Population*
Karl Marx's *Capital*
Thomas Piketty's *Capital in the Twenty-First Century*
Amartya Sen's *Development as Freedom*
Adam Smith's *The Wealth of Nations*
Nassim Nicholas Taleb's *The Black Swan: The Impact of the Highly Improbable*
Amos Tversky's & Daniel Kahneman's *Judgment under Uncertainty: Heuristics and Biases*
Mahbub Ul Haq's *Reflections on Human Development*
Max Weber's *The Protestant Ethic and the Spirit of Capitalism*

FEMINISM AND GENDER STUDIES

Judith Butler's *Gender Trouble*
Simone De Beauvoir's *The Second Sex*
Michel Foucault's *History of Sexuality*
Betty Friedan's *The Feminine Mystique*
Saba Mahmood's *The Politics of Piety: The Islamic Revival and the Feminist Subject*
Joan Wallach Scott's *Gender and the Politics of History*
Mary Wollstonecraft's *A Vindication of the Rights of Woman*
Virginia Woolf's *A Room of One's Own*

GEOGRAPHY

The Brundtland Report's *Our Common Future*
Rachel Carson's *Silent Spring*
Charles Darwin's *On the Origin of Species*
James Ferguson's *The Anti-Politics Machine*
Jane Jacobs's *The Death and Life of Great American Cities*
James Lovelock's *Gaia: A New Look at Life on Earth*
Amartya Sen's *Development as Freedom*
Mathis Wackernagel & William Rees's *Our Ecological Footprint*

HISTORY

Janet Abu-Lughod's *Before European Hegemony*
Benedict Anderson's *Imagined Communities*
Bernard Bailyn's *The Ideological Origins of the American Revolution*
Hanna Batatu's *The Old Social Classes And The Revolutionary Movements Of Iraq*
Christopher Browning's *Ordinary Men: Reserve Police Batallion 101 and the Final Solution in Poland*
Edmund Burke's *Reflections on the Revolution in France*
William Cronon's *Nature's Metropolis: Chicago And The Great West*
Alfred W. Crosby's *The Columbian Exchange*
Hamid Dabashi's *Iran: A People Interrupted*
David Brion Davis's *The Problem of Slavery in the Age of Revolution*
Nathalie Zemon Davis's *The Return of Martin Guerre*
Jared Diamond's *Guns, Germs & Steel: the Fate of Human Societies*
Frank Dikotter's *Mao's Great Famine*
John W Dower's *War Without Mercy: Race And Power In The Pacific War*
W. E. B. Du Bois's *The Souls of Black Folk*
Richard J. Evans's *In Defence of History*
Lucien Febvre's *The Problem of Unbelief in the 16th Century*
Sheila Fitzpatrick's *Everyday Stalinism*

The Macat Library By Discipline

Eric Foner's *Reconstruction: America's Unfinished Revolution, 1863-1877*
Michel Foucault's *Discipline and Punish*
Michel Foucault's *History of Sexuality*
Francis Fukuyama's *The End of History and the Last Man*
John Lewis Gaddis's *We Now Know: Rethinking Cold War History*
Ernest Gellner's *Nations and Nationalism*
Eugene Genovese's *Roll, Jordan, Roll: The World the Slaves Made*
Carlo Ginzburg's *The Night Battles*
Daniel Goldhagen's *Hitler's Willing Executioners*
Jack Goldstone's *Revolution and Rebellion in the Early Modern World*
Antonio Gramsci's *The Prison Notebooks*
Alexander Hamilton, John Jay & James Madison's *The Federalist Papers*
Christopher Hill's *The World Turned Upside Down*
Carole Hillenbrand's *The Crusades: Islamic Perspectives*
Thomas Hobbes's *Leviathan*
Eric Hobsbawm's *The Age Of Revolution*
John A. Hobson's *Imperialism: A Study*
Albert Hourani's *History of the Arab Peoples*
Samuel P. Huntington's *The Clash of Civilizations and the Remaking of World Order*
C. L. R. James's *The Black Jacobins*
Tony Judt's *Postwar: A History of Europe Since 1945*
Ernst Kantorowicz's *The King's Two Bodies: A Study in Medieval Political Theology*
Paul Kennedy's *The Rise and Fall of the Great Powers*
Ian Kershaw's *The "Hitler Myth": Image and Reality in the Third Reich*
John Maynard Keynes's *The General Theory of Employment, Interest and Money*
Charles P. Kindleberger's *Manias, Panics and Crashes*
Martin Luther King Jr's *Why We Can't Wait*
Henry Kissinger's *World Order: Reflections on the Character of Nations and the Course of History*
Thomas Kuhn's *The Structure of Scientific Revolutions*
Georges Lefebvre's *The Coming of the French Revolution*
John Locke's *Two Treatises of Government*
Niccolò Machiavelli's *The Prince*
Thomas Robert Malthus's *An Essay on the Principle of Population*
Mahmood Mamdani's *Citizen and Subject: Contemporary Africa And The Legacy Of Late Colonialism*
Karl Marx's *Capital*
Stanley Milgram's *Obedience to Authority*
John Stuart Mill's *On Liberty*
Thomas Paine's *Common Sense*
Thomas Paine's *Rights of Man*
Geoffrey Parker's *Global Crisis: War, Climate Change and Catastrophe in the Seventeenth Century*
Jonathan Riley-Smith's *The First Crusade and the Idea of Crusading*
Jean-Jacques Rousseau's *The Social Contract*
Joan Wallach Scott's *Gender and the Politics of History*
Theda Skocpol's *States and Social Revolutions*
Adam Smith's *The Wealth of Nations*
Timothy Snyder's *Bloodlands: Europe Between Hitler and Stalin*
Sun Tzu's *The Art of War*
Keith Thomas's *Religion and the Decline of Magic*
Thucydides's *The History of the Peloponnesian War*
Frederick Jackson Turner's *The Significance of the Frontier in American History*
Odd Arne Westad's *The Global Cold War: Third World Interventions And The Making Of Our Times*

LITERATURE

Chinua Achebe's *An Image of Africa: Racism in Conrad's Heart of Darkness*
Roland Barthes's *Mythologies*
Homi K. Bhabha's *The Location of Culture*
Judith Butler's *Gender Trouble*
Simone De Beauvoir's *The Second Sex*
Ferdinand De Saussure's *Course in General Linguistics*
T. S. Eliot's *The Sacred Wood: Essays on Poetry and Criticism*
Zora Neale Huston's *Characteristics of Negro Expression*
Toni Morrison's *Playing in the Dark: Whiteness in the American Literary Imagination*
Edward Said's *Orientalism*
Gayatri Chakravorty Spivak's *Can the Subaltern Speak?*
Mary Wollstonecraft's *A Vindication of the Rights of Women*
Virginia Woolf's *A Room of One's Own*

PHILOSOPHY

Elizabeth Anscombe's *Modern Moral Philosophy*
Hannah Arendt's *The Human Condition*
Aristotle's *Metaphysics*
Aristotle's *Nicomachean Ethics*
Edmund Gettier's *Is Justified True Belief Knowledge?*
Georg Wilhelm Friedrich Hegel's *Phenomenology of Spirit*
David Hume's *Dialogues Concerning Natural Religion*
David Hume's *The Enquiry for Human Understanding*
Immanuel Kant's *Religion within the Boundaries of Mere Reason*
Immanuel Kant's *Critique of Pure Reason*
Søren Kierkegaard's *The Sickness Unto Death*
Søren Kierkegaard's *Fear and Trembling*
C. S. Lewis's *The Abolition of Man*
Alasdair MacIntyre's *After Virtue*
Marcus Aurelius's *Meditations*
Friedrich Nietzsche's *On the Genealogy of Morality*
Friedrich Nietzsche's *Beyond Good and Evil*
Plato's *Republic*
Plato's *Symposium*
Jean-Jacques Rousseau's *The Social Contract*
Gilbert Ryle's *The Concept of Mind*
Baruch Spinoza's *Ethics*
Sun Tzu's *The Art of War*
Ludwig Wittgenstein's *Philosophical Investigations*

POLITICS

Benedict Anderson's *Imagined Communities*
Aristotle's *Politics*
Bernard Bailyn's *The Ideological Origins of the American Revolution*
Edmund Burke's *Reflections on the Revolution in France*
John C. Calhoun's *A Disquisition on Government*
Ha-Joon Chang's *Kicking Away the Ladder*
Hamid Dabashi's *Iran: A People Interrupted*
Hamid Dabashi's *Theology of Discontent: The Ideological Foundation of the Islamic Revolution in Iran*
Robert Dahl's *Democracy and its Critics*
Robert Dahl's *Who Governs?*
David Brion Davis's *The Problem of Slavery in the Age of Revolution*

The Macat Library By Discipline

Alexis De Tocqueville's *Democracy in America*
James Ferguson's *The Anti-Politics Machine*
Frank Dikotter's *Mao's Great Famine*
Sheila Fitzpatrick's *Everyday Stalinism*
Eric Foner's *Reconstruction: America's Unfinished Revolution, 1863-1877*
Milton Friedman's *Capitalism and Freedom*
Francis Fukuyama's *The End of History and the Last Man*
John Lewis Gaddis's *We Now Know: Rethinking Cold War History*
Ernest Gellner's *Nations and Nationalism*
David Graeber's *Debt: the First 5000 Years*
Antonio Gramsci's *The Prison Notebooks*
Alexander Hamilton, John Jay & James Madison's *The Federalist Papers*
Friedrich Hayek's *The Road to Serfdom*
Christopher Hill's *The World Turned Upside Down*
Thomas Hobbes's *Leviathan*
John A. Hobson's *Imperialism: A Study*
Samuel P. Huntington's *The Clash of Civilizations and the Remaking of World Order*
Tony Judt's *Postwar: A History of Europe Since 1945*
David C. Kang's *China Rising: Peace, Power and Order in East Asia*
Paul Kennedy's *The Rise and Fall of Great Powers*
Robert Keohane's *After Hegemony*
Martin Luther King Jr.'s *Why We Can't Wait*
Henry Kissinger's *World Order: Reflections on the Character of Nations and the Course of History*
John Locke's *Two Treatises of Government*
Niccolò Machiavelli's *The Prince*
Thomas Robert Malthus's *An Essay on the Principle of Population*
Mahmood Mamdani's *Citizen and Subject: Contemporary Africa And The Legacy Of Late Colonialism*
Karl Marx's *Capital*
John Stuart Mill's *On Liberty*
John Stuart Mill's *Utilitarianism*
Hans Morgenthau's *Politics Among Nations*
Thomas Paine's *Common Sense*
Thomas Paine's *Rights of Man*
Thomas Piketty's *Capital in the Twenty-First Century*
Robert D. Putman's *Bowling Alone*
John Rawls's *Theory of Justice*
Jean-Jacques Rousseau's *The Social Contract*
Theda Skocpol's *States and Social Revolutions*
Adam Smith's *The Wealth of Nations*
Sun Tzu's *The Art of War*
Henry David Thoreau's *Civil Disobedience*
Thucydides's *The History of the Peloponnesian War*
Kenneth Waltz's *Theory of International Politics*
Max Weber's *Politics as a Vocation*
Odd Arne Westad's *The Global Cold War: Third World Interventions And The Making Of Our Times*

POSTCOLONIAL STUDIES

Roland Barthes's *Mythologies*
Frantz Fanon's *Black Skin, White Masks*
Homi K. Bhabha's *The Location of Culture*
Gustavo Gutiérrez's *A Theology of Liberation*
Edward Said's *Orientalism*
Gayatri Chakravorty Spivak's *Can the Subaltern Speak?*

PSYCHOLOGY

Gordon Allport's *The Nature of Prejudice*
Alan Baddeley & Graham Hitch's *Aggression: A Social Learning Analysis*
Albert Bandura's *Aggression: A Social Learning Analysis*
Leon Festinger's *A Theory of Cognitive Dissonance*
Sigmund Freud's *The Interpretation of Dreams*
Betty Friedan's *The Feminine Mystique*
Michael R. Gottfredson & Travis Hirschi's *A General Theory of Crime*
Eric Hoffer's *The True Believer: Thoughts on the Nature of Mass Movements*
William James's *Principles of Psychology*
Elizabeth Loftus's *Eyewitness Testimony*
A. H. Maslow's *A Theory of Human Motivation*
Stanley Milgram's *Obedience to Authority*
Steven Pinker's *The Better Angels of Our Nature*
Oliver Sacks's *The Man Who Mistook His Wife For a Hat*
Richard Thaler & Cass Sunstein's *Nudge: Improving Decisions About Health, Wealth and Happiness*
Amos Tversky's *Judgment under Uncertainty: Heuristics and Biases*
Philip Zimbardo's *The Lucifer Effect*

SCIENCE

Rachel Carson's *Silent Spring*
William Cronon's *Nature's Metropolis: Chicago And The Great West*
Alfred W. Crosby's *The Columbian Exchange*
Charles Darwin's *On the Origin of Species*
Richard Dawkin's *The Selfish Gene*
Thomas Kuhn's *The Structure of Scientific Revolutions*
Geoffrey Parker's *Global Crisis: War, Climate Change and Catastrophe in the Seventeenth Century*
Mathis Wackernagel & William Rees's *Our Ecological Footprint*

SOCIOLOGY

Michelle Alexander's *The New Jim Crow: Mass Incarceration in the Age of Colorblindness*
Gordon Allport's *The Nature of Prejudice*
Albert Bandura's *Aggression: A Social Learning Analysis*
Hanna Batatu's *The Old Social Classes And The Revolutionary Movements Of Iraq*
Ha-Joon Chang's *Kicking Away the Ladder*
W. E. B. Du Bois's *The Souls of Black Folk*
Émile Durkheim's *On Suicide*
Frantz Fanon's *Black Skin, White Masks*
Frantz Fanon's *The Wretched of the Earth*
Eric Foner's *Reconstruction: America's Unfinished Revolution, 1863-1877*
Eugene Genovese's *Roll, Jordan, Roll: The World the Slaves Made*
Jack Goldstone's *Revolution and Rebellion in the Early Modern World*
Antonio Gramsci's *The Prison Notebooks*
Richard Herrnstein & Charles A Murray's *The Bell Curve: Intelligence and Class Structure in American Life*
Eric Hoffer's *The True Believer: Thoughts on the Nature of Mass Movements*
Jane Jacobs's *The Death and Life of Great American Cities*
Robert Lucas's *Why Doesn't Capital Flow from Rich to Poor Countries?*
Jay Macleod's *Ain't No Makin' It: Aspirations and Attainment in a Low Income Neighborhood*
Elaine May's *Homeward Bound: American Families in the Cold War Era*
Douglas McGregor's *The Human Side of Enterprise*
C. Wright Mills's *The Sociological Imagination*

The Macat Library By Discipline

Thomas Piketty's *Capital in the Twenty-First Century*
Robert D. Putman's *Bowling Alone*
David Riesman's *The Lonely Crowd: A Study of the Changing American Character*
Edward Said's *Orientalism*
Joan Wallach Scott's *Gender and the Politics of History*
Theda Skocpol's *States and Social Revolutions*
Max Weber's *The Protestant Ethic and the Spirit of Capitalism*

THEOLOGY

Augustine's *Confessions*
Benedict's *Rule of St Benedict*
Gustavo Gutiérrez's *A Theology of Liberation*
Carole Hillenbrand's *The Crusades: Islamic Perspectives*
David Hume's *Dialogues Concerning Natural Religion*
Immanuel Kant's *Religion within the Boundaries of Mere Reason*
Ernst Kantorowicz's *The King's Two Bodies: A Study in Medieval Political Theology*
Søren Kierkegaard's *The Sickness Unto Death*
C. S. Lewis's *The Abolition of Man*
Saba Mahmood's *The Politics of Piety: The Islamic Revival and the Feminist Subject*
Baruch Spinoza's *Ethics*
Keith Thomas's *Religion and the Decline of Magic*

COMING SOON

Chris Argyris's *The Individual and the Organisation*
Seyla Benhabib's *The Rights of Others*
Walter Benjamin's *The Work Of Art in the Age of Mechanical Reproduction*
John Berger's *Ways of Seeing*
Pierre Bourdieu's *Outline of a Theory of Practice*
Mary Douglas's *Purity and Danger*
Roland Dworkin's *Taking Rights Seriously*
James G. March's *Exploration and Exploitation in Organisational Learning*
Ikujiro Nonaka's *A Dynamic Theory of Organizational Knowledge Creation*
Griselda Pollock's *Vision and Difference*
Amartya Sen's *Inequality Re-Examined*
Susan Sontag's *On Photography*
Yasser Tabbaa's *The Transformation of Islamic Art*
Ludwig von Mises's *Theory of Money and Credit*

Macat Disciplines

Access the greatest ideas and thinkers across entire disciplines, including

AFRICANA STUDIES

Chinua Achebe's *An Image of Africa: Racism in Conrad's Heart of Darkness*

W. E. B. Du Bois's *The Souls of Black Folk*

Zora Neale Hurston's *Characteristics of Negro Expression*

Martin Luther King Jr.'s *Why We Can't Wait*

Toni Morrison's *Playing in the Dark: Whiteness in the American Literary Imagination*

Macat analyses are available from all good bookshops and libraries.

Access hundreds of analyses through one, multimedia tool.
Join free for one month **library.macat.com**

Macat Disciplines

Access the greatest ideas and thinkers across entire disciplines, including

FEMINISM, GENDER AND QUEER STUDIES

Simone De Beauvoir's
The Second Sex

Michel Foucault's
History of Sexuality

Betty Friedan's
The Feminine Mystique

Saba Mahmood's
*The Politics of Piety:
The Islamic Revival and
the Feminist Subject*

Joan Wallach Scott's
*Gender and the
Politics of History*

Mary Wollstonecraft's
*A Vindication of the
Rights of Woman*

Virginia Woolf's
A Room of One's Own

Judith Butler's
Gender Trouble

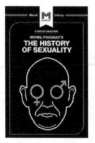

Macat analyses are available from all good bookshops and libraries.

Access hundreds of analyses through one, multimedia tool.
Join free for one month **library.macat.com**

Macat Disciplines

Access the greatest ideas and thinkers across entire disciplines, including

INEQUALITY

Ha-Joon Chang's, *Kicking Away the Ladder*

David Graeber's, *Debt: The First 5000 Years*

Robert E. Lucas's, *Why Doesn't Capital Flow from Rich To Poor Countries?*

Thomas Piketty's, *Capital in the Twenty-First Century*

Amartya Sen's, *Inequality Re-Examined*

Mahbub Ul Haq's, *Reflections on Human Development*

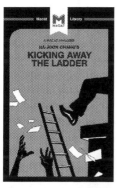

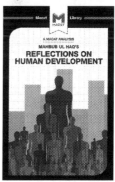

Macat analyses are available from all good bookshops and libraries.

Access hundreds of analyses through one, multimedia tool.
Join free for one month **library.macat.com**

Macat Disciplines

Access the greatest ideas and thinkers across entire disciplines, including

CRIMINOLOGY

Michelle Alexander's
The New Jim Crow: Mass Incarceration in the Age of Colorblindness

Michael R. Gottfredson & Travis Hirschi's
A General Theory of Crime

Elizabeth Loftus's
Eyewitness Testimony

Richard Herrnstein & Charles A. Murray's
The Bell Curve: Intelligence and Class Structure in American Life

Jay Macleod's
Ain't No Makin' It: Aspirations and Attainment in a Low-Income Neighborhood

Philip Zimbardo's
The Lucifer Effect

Macat analyses are available from all good bookshops and libraries.

Access hundreds of analyses through one, multimedia tool.
Join free for one month **library.macat.com**

Macat Disciplines

Access the greatest ideas and thinkers across entire disciplines, including

Postcolonial Studies

Roland Barthes's *Mythologies*
Frantz Fanon's *Black Skin, White Masks*
Homi K. Bhabha's *The Location of Culture*
Gustavo Gutiérrez's *A Theology of Liberation*
Edward Said's *Orientalism*
Gayatri Chakravorty Spivak's *Can the Subaltern Speak?*

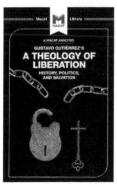
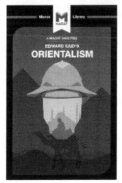

Macat analyses are available from all good bookshops and libraries.

Access hundreds of analyses through one, multimedia tool.
Join free for one month **library.macat.com**

Macat Disciplines

Access the greatest ideas and thinkers across entire disciplines, including

GLOBALIZATION

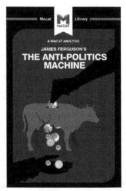

Arjun Appadurai's, *Modernity at Large: Cultural Dimensions of Globalisation*

James Ferguson's, *The Anti-Politics Machine*

Geert Hofstede's, *Culture's Consequences*

Amartya Sen's, *Development as Freedom*

Macat analyses are available from all good bookshops and libraries.

Access hundreds of analyses through one, multimedia tool.
Join free for one month **library.macat.com**

Macat Pairs

Analyse historical and modern issues
from opposite sides of an argument.
Pairs include:

HOW TO RUN AN ECONOMY

John Maynard Keynes's
The General Theory OF Employment,
Interest and Money

Classical economics suggests that market economies are self-correcting in times of recession or depression, and tend toward full employment and output. But English economist John Maynard Keynes disagrees.

In his ground-breaking 1936 study *The General Theory*, Keynes argues that traditional economics has misunderstood the causes of unemployment. Employment is not determined by the price of labor; it is directly linked to demand. Keynes believes market economies are by nature unstable, and so require government intervention. Spurred on by the social catastrophe of the Great Depression of the 1930s, he sets out to revolutionize the way the world thinks

Milton Friedman's
The Role of Monetary Policy

Friedman's 1968 paper changed the course of economic theory. In just 17 pages, he demolished existing theory and outlined an effective alternate monetary policy designed to secure 'high employment, stable prices and rapid growth.'

Friedman demonstrated that monetary policy plays a vital role in broader economic stability and argued that economists got their monetary policy wrong in the 1950s and 1960s by misunderstanding the relationship between inflation and unemployment. Previous generations of economists had believed that governments could permanently decrease unemployment by permitting inflation—and vice versa. Friedman's most original contribution was to show that this supposed trade-off is an illusion that only works in the short term.

Macat analyses are available from all good bookshops and libraries.

Access hundreds of analyses through one, multimedia tool.
Join free for one month **library.macat.com**

Printed in the United States
by Baker & Taylor Publisher Services